Ask Me About My Grandcats

And other comedy essays

Michael Jenkins

For you. And you.

Contents

A Follow-Up Fan Letter to Tom Petty 10

You're Cordially Invited to the Anderson Monthly
Neighborhood Orgy!...15

Let's Paint the Nursery 19

A Bystander From A Lethal Weapon 2 Chase
Scene Arrives Home...23

I Interview Andrew McCarthy 26

As a Clairvoyant, I am Able to--Hey, Where're
You Going?...31

The Unappreciated, Aspiring Author Files an Auto
Insurance Claim...34

This Vacuum Salesman Can't Believe Your Family
Isn't Already Fucking Dead...............................37

Advice Column: Ask Charles Bukowski...................40

Another Slow Day at the Suicide Prevention
Center 43

The Ultimate Way...46

I Believe This Book You Lent Me Has Spent Some
Considerable Time in Your Bathroom......................49

Catalogue Writer's Block 52

What I'd Say to my Crewmates if I were In Cortez's Army and He Just Purposely Sank Our Ships...55

Aw, Man! Rudy Found a Dumpster Baby..............60

How DOMINO'S 2 for 1 Medium Pizza Deal (limit one topping) Saved My Marriage.................................64

I Interview Jim Rome..69

I'm Sure Mathew Broderick Still Sometimes Feels Bad About Those Two People He Ran Over in 1987...73

Setting the Doomsday Clock 77

My Last Day Teaching Kindergarten 85

Jesus, How am I Going to Segue This Story of a Raped and Killed 7-Year-Old Girl Over to the Weekend Weather Report?...89

Welcome to the Fleshlight Family!............................91

That Clock is Slow, Just Like Your Son....................94

To Whoever Was Using This Glory Hole 97

...And You Can Tell Mr. Phelps I'm Way Too Cowardly to Say These Things to His Face! 101

Oprah Interviews the Author of This Book 104

Greetings From the Nickelback Fan Club!............109

Welcome to the Office, Champ 113

Alright, Which One of you Assholes Stole My Jock Jams Volume II CD? 116

Before We Begin 119

Advice Column: Ask a Premature Ejaculator 122

I Interview Jake Steinfeld, A.K.A Body By Jake.124

So, I'm Thinking About Getting a Leg Tattoo 129

Steve Guttenberg Contemplates Reprising His Role For Short Circuit 2.......................................133

Pullin' the Pud: That Chick From the Progressive Insurance Commercials, Flo 136

Does This Feel Contagious To You? 140

Your Cousins Are Hot, Dude 143

A Lovely Little Dinner Party 147

We Need to Talk About Kevin 151

Well, Excuse me, *Doctor,* But If Urine is So Sterile, Why Do I Feel Sick Every Time I Drink it?............155

You Guys Remember When I Lost My Arm That One Time?..159

This Condolence Card Should Add Just the Right Amount of Sexual Tension...............................162

Welcome to Kmart Layaway, You Depress the Ever-Loving Shit Out of Me!.............................165

Bruce Merriweather: Lyrical Fact-Checker.........168

What is That Stuff in Your Ear and What Can We, As a Society, Do About It? 174

I Interview Neil Clark Warren, Founder of EHarmony 180

Man, This Stripper Is All *Over* Me 185

Ask Me About My Grandcats.................................188

This Relationship Was Much More Romantic When You Were In That Coma................................190

If Craig T. Nelson Were My Uncle, I Think I'd Be Terrified Pretty Much All of the Time 193

Looks Like That Dim-Witted Boy From up the Street is Discovering the Hornet's Nest Out Front 200

No, Wait-- NOW is the Best Time to Buy a Kia!..208

The Obvious Logistical Nightmare of Making Smurf Porn 212

I'd Like to Return This Baby in a Jar, Please 216

Thanks for the Hospitality...221

If My Boss, Mr. Shirley, Gave the Eulogy at My Funeral..225

The Self-Published Acceptance Letter 229

A Follow-Up Fan Letter to Tom Petty

Dear Mr. Petty,

You rock! My name is Mike Jenkins and I am writing you to follow up on a fan-letter that I wrote to you a while back. When I first sent off the letter, I figured that it would take at least three days for the fan letter to reach you, another two or three days for you to sort through the mail and fashion a response, and another three days for the letter to get back to me in Pennsylvania. Sadly, however, I have not yet received a response from you, which will be 24 years ago next week.

After 24 years of patient waiting (that's the hardest part, am I right, Tom?) I proffered the idea that you actually might not get back to me and I would like to write this letter to plead that if you have decided not to write me back, please reconsider. Even though I am not 9 years old anymore, I would still be the happiest boy in the world if you responded to my original letter.

I know that at the time of writing my first letter to you, you and the Heartbreakers were gearing up for your "Into the Great Wide Open" tour and you were probably much too busy to be reading (let alone responding to) fan mail. I understood that, even though I was secretly hoping that you would announce my name at your concert in Philadelphia at the Spectrum, which was my first concert, by the way. The concert, of course, totally rocked.

Some interesting things have happened while waiting for your response, Mr. Petty. When I was 10, I saw my friend's older sister in just her jeans and a bra. It's true, Tom! I was walking down the hallway of my friend's house and she was standing there with the door open and when she saw me looking at her, she slammed the door in my face. The bra was white, in case I didn't paint a vivid enough image for you.

Have you ever seen a girl in a bra, Tom? It's wild, let me tell ya!

Nothing much else has happened for me since then while I've been waiting for your letter. I got strep throat a couple times and I bought a couple more of your albums. I didn't expect the bra moment to be the peak of my entire life, but then again, I was also expecting you to write me back, which would have topped the bra moment by leaps and bounds, no doubt about it! But people get busy, I understand.

I am a busy person myself. I have a hermit crab that depends on me to survive. I got him 6 months ago at the local pet store while I was waiting for your letter. In that same trip, I also picked up your 30-year anniversary documentary that was directed by Peter Bogdanovich. It was an incredible movie, even though I was kind of half-hoping that you would mention my letter, but it's okay that you didn't.

In the documentary, however, I did notice that you got in contact with one of your fans and visited him. His name was Eddie Veddar and you sang with him on stage. It may very well have been the highlight of his career, if not life. And that got me to thinking: perhaps you would like to come and visit me at *my* place of employment!

Don't be so quick to dismiss the notion, Mr. Petty. I work in a small machine shop where we cut rolls of plastic film down from one size to other various custom sizes. I run a machine that's bigger than my living room/kitchen area and this massive machine has two buttons, a red one and a green one. Are you curious which one does which? Well, no spoilers! You're going to have to come over here to find out.

And the answer may surprise you!

If you would feel more comfortable wearing a guitar while we run the machine, maybe even don your harmonica rack as well, I can talk to my supervisor and see if we can work something out. I don't think it will be a problem. But one thing that I know we can't budge on is wearing a hairnet; everybody has to wear hairnets, Tom. Hey, I don't like it either, but rules are rules. We do, however, get a couple of 10 minute breaks where we can go out to the parking lot and talk about stuff. I think it is during these 10 minute breaks where we will get to become friends.

I'm sorry, I got off-track. Inviting you to my workplace was not the sole intent of this letter. If you find my original fan letter from 1991, I'm sure you'll notice that I said my favorite song of yours was "Spike" from your 1985 *Southern Accents* album. Well, after giving it 24 years of thought and patient waiting, I've decided that "Spike" is no longer my favorite song. I'm sorry to throw you such a wicked curveball, but I think when I told you that 24 years ago, I was trying really hard to be different, to stand out from the crowd; to show you that I'm a real fan by nominating one of the deeper cuts to show you I meant business. But as time goes on I realize I can be honest with you and tell you that my favorite song is "Shadow of a Doubt (A Complex Kid)" from your *Damn the Torpedoes* album.

What a relief! I'm so glad I told you that! So, please, take this new information into consideration when you (finally) write me back. Thank you very much for your time, Mr. Petty.

Your number 1 fan,

Mike Jenkins

You're Cordially Invited to the Anderson Monthly Neighborhood Orgy!

Greetings and salutations, folks! Larry and Mary Anderson here, wishing you a happy month of July. If you are receiving this letter, then you know what that means: the monthly neighborhood orgy is right around the corner and we would like to see you there!

When: August 16th, 10:00 pm.

Where: Larry and Mary's bungalow, of course!

Theme: Justice League (Superman, Batman, Bloodwynd... Get creative!)

Mary and I would like to apologize for being unable to make an orgy for the month of July, but there was just so much going on concerning family vacations, not to mention Mary's mother ("Old Ironsides," as I call her) coming to town for the better part of the week, as well as our grandkids birthdays... there was just no time to get into a huge pile and have sex with each other.

June's gathering was a successful one, as usual, but there were some comments and concerns in the suggestion box that I would like to address.

Ok, first point of discussion: No pets. I cannot believe how many times I have to address this particular topic. And this message is really for Gary, in all honesty. Gary, when we had our first monthly meeting, you brought a dog with you, and I was like, "Ok, Gary, Haha, very funny, but no pets, buddy." Then you proceeded to bring a different animal to *every single* gathering since. What was it last time? A frog? Yeah, it was a frog. Where do I even start with that? Like, where would a frog possibly fit into the *Star Wars* themed orgy we had last month? Is this a running site gag with you now? I wish you would knock it off, Gary. Honestly.

Secondly, there seems to be a habit of people scampering off immediately after they have finished. I notice this mostly with the men. Guys, it is seen as pretty rude to run out the door immediately after you have had your fun. We may all be wearing masks and whatnot, but we can still tell who is bolting toward the door immediately after gratification. I mean, it's not like we are asking you to spend the night or anything, but stick around for a bit, ya know? Relax! Have a cup of coffee or a glass of wine when you are done and put your feet up; I would love to show you some slides that Mary and I took on our vacation to Daytona Beach last year. You can even take your mask off by that point if you would like. No pressure.

And lastly, this suggestion does not come from the suggestion box, but rather from me: guys, you have to bring your wives. I cannot emphasize this enough. If you are invited to this orgy, it is because you are a part of a couple, and Mary and I expect both of you to show up to the event. It seems that in the month of May, every guy there had an excuse as to why their wives could not show up. Excuses ranged from "that time of the month," to "tuberculosis," to "hay fever." At first I didn't say anything, but then for last month's meeting, the same thing happened. I don't know if I made this abundantly clear or not, but this is a *swingers' orgy*, okay? I don't want to get into semantics here, but what has been happening the last two meetings is about 10 or 11 guys and one woman, and that is not an orgy, okay? That is something else entirely. And don't get me wrong; Mary loved the attention. She was very flattered by it, but it comes with a physical toll that very few have ever known. So, guys, if you find yourself on August 16th standing at our front door, make sure your wife is with you before you give us a knock, mmkay?

I know if we can abide by these standards we will all have an excellent time. Thank you for hearing me out. If you would like to bring an adult film to put on in the background, we do have VHS capabilities as well as Beta. Personally, I don't know why you would bring that to an orgy. If you go to a rock concert, do you bring your Walkman? But hey, we're open to it. You don't hold this many orgies if you weren't a little open-minded, know what I mean?

If you are interested in bringing something to the orgy food-wise, try to avoid problem foods such as: sauerkraut, deviled eggs, or anything cabbage-related. And yes, Mary will be making her famous lemon squares for the orgy. So come for the lemon squares, stay for the orgy. Or vice-versa! Nyuk nyuk! We hope to see you then!

Respectfully,

Larry and Mary

P.s.-- We also just acquired a brand new, top-of-the-line dehumidifier for the living room, so for the person who commented that by the end of the orgy our house smelled like, "lemon squared ass," you should know that the stank should no longer be a problem. Toodles!

Let's Paint the Nursery

Alright, Todd, here I am, ready to help you paint this nursery. Have you figured out if you and Christine are going to have a boy or a girl? You don't want to know? What a gamble! Have you ever painted a room before? It's ok, it's nothing to be embarrassed about. To be honest, I don't really have that much experience either. I do recall the one or two times I helped my dad paint my room as a kid. He showed me the 6 simplest steps it takes to paint a room and I've been looking for a time where I get to try it out myself. I was also wondering if I could use your name when I write about this in my blog. No? Well, what if I sweetened the pot and told you that nobody reads it anyway? Still no? You're a tough nut to crack, Todd. We'll do it your way. Okay, let's go with step number one. According to my dad, we should...

Step #1- "Hand Me That Beer"
Todd, you got any beer? I don't care how early in the morning it is, my dad always had me handing him a beer before he started any project

around the house, *especially* when he painted. Well, how many do you have in the fridge? Can Christine go out and get some more? I figure with a room this size, we're going to need at least... 4 beers apiece. And before you ask, no, I don't have any money. Tell Christine to get some more beer and we can start after we take the ones from the fridge. Of course I have a bottle opener! Look who you're talking to, guy!

Step #2- "Stir the Paint With a Paint Stick. No, Not With Your Hand, Don't Be Retarded"

Tater Todd, it's crucial that we stir the paint with these wooden sticks you got at the store. If you use the length of your arm to do it, the paint sticks like you wouldn't believe and it molds itself to every individual hair and you basically have to scrub it all off with a brillo pad while my dad stands next to you and calls you a retard. And I don't want to call you a retard, Tates. So, if we can both safely use the sticks to stir the paint, then we're not retarded, okay? I'm saving you a lot of mental and physical anguish here.

Step #3- "What Color is This? Yellow? You Want Your Room Yellow? What Are You, Some Kind of a Homo?"

Since you don't know if it's a boy or a girl, what color did you decide to go with? Or are you just going to roll the dice and paint it blue? Oh! Orange! That's a good choice. It's more masculine than say, yellow, I guess. Yellow has a bad stigma with it for some reason. Personally, I always thought it was a happy color, yellow. But I guess some people don't feel that way. But orange! Orange is good. It's bold, confident. You made a good choice with the orange. I don't know much about colors, I just know that some people *really* don't like to paint rooms yellow.

Step #4- "Don't Be an Idiot"

Todd, let's skip Step #4 and see if this paint tastes as good as it smells. C'mon, aren't you curious what orange tastes like? I am! I know for a fact that yellow doesn't taste like sunshine, but maybe orange tastes like oranges; don't know until you try, all I'm saying.

Step #5- "No, Brush it Up And Down in Even Strokes, Not Side to Side. No, I Said NOT Side to Side! Whatsa Matter With You? Are You Deaf or Just Stupid? (Sigh) Just Give Me the Brush."

Todd, I've found that painting a wall in horizontal strokes creates a very hostile environment and I don't want your child raised in such an atmosphere. Allow me to impart some wisdom on you: vertical paint strokes are where it's at! Painting vertically will basically be your last chance at redemption before reaching the final step, Step 6.

Step #6- "Why Don't You Go Downstairs and Help Your Mother in the Kitchen?"

Hey, where is Christine? Is she downstairs? I can help her with whatever she's doing. In fact, why don't I go see if she's doing okay? So what if we haven't gotten anything done? You stay up here and get to work. I don't know exactly how it works, but all I have to do for Step 6 is leave a six pack of beer outside the door every few hours and by the end of the day the room is done. That's basically how you paint a room, as far as I know. I'll leave a sixer by the door and the room should be finished by 2:00 or so. Good luck!

A Bystander From A Lethal Weapon 2 Chase Scene Arrives Home

Hi, honey, I'm home. You will not *believe* the day I had today! It was the most insane thing I have ever seen. No, I'm sorry, I didn't get to pick up the milk on the way back. Listen: the cops chased down and killed some guy on the construction site today. I know!

They never told us who the guy was or what he did, but I'm getting ahead of myself. There I was, doing the timber framing, getting the site ready for the pavers. I was setting the cruck in just the right position, when Bill goes, "Hey, did you hear that?" And I don't. I figure Bill is just screwing with me. You know how Bill is. No, Bill Thompson. He and his wife came over for dinner a couple months back. You said his wife was kind of snarky. Yeah, that Bill. So, anyway, I start to hear something all the sudden, like impending doom. We look at each other, and the sound gets louder: there're car horns honking, there's screaming, a little bit of gunfire, and just when it couldn't get any louder... silence. We look up and there is this goddamn car in sky, like, in slow motion, flying off the beltway above us.

I heard silence when that thing was coming toward us. Bill said he heard a waning saxophone playing, but I think he was just in shock.

It's incredible, right? So we both grab ahold of each other and jump out of the way while this fucking car comes crashing down. It falls right through all of the framing and joint work we had been setting up for weeks. Hours and hours of work--gone.

The driver, he's dead, and the guy who took the fall with the car, he dislocates his goddamn shoulder, and he's running around looking for a beam to slam his shoulder into. We're all looking at each other, like, "What the fuck," right? So he starts slamming his shoulder into the beam and then this old black guy shows up in this beat-up station wagon, and he's like, "Hey, yo, Riggs! Riggs!"

It turns out this guy was a cop! We didn't know what to make of the whole thing. They were chasing some suspicious-looking guy and it ended right on our site. So this Riggs guy, he pops his shoulder back in and he and the black guy limp off to the car, bicker back and forth like an old married couple, and then drive away!

And we're all like, "…the fuck?"

That all happened at around 1:00. You know what we were doing the whole rest of the day? Filing reports with the other cops who showed up minutes later. I was asking around, and it turns out that this Riggs guy is a real wild card. He plays it fast and loose, apparently. Word on the street is that the captain is really on his ass and his partner's ass to get a break in the case they're working on. Personally, and I say this in the hopes that you won't tell anyone this, but this Riggs's guy hair was absolutely *amazing!* It was like a flowing mane of masculinity and badassery. Don't tell Bill I said that though, ok?

If I were the captain, I would be on Riggs's ass too, because our foreman, Terry, he said he is going to sue the city because of all the progress we lost today. So now the mayor is going to be on the captain's ass and the captain is on Riggs's ass…everybody is on everybody else's ass, apparently.

No, it means overtime for guys like me and Bill, so that's a good thing. I just hope Riggs and Murtaugh (that was his partner's name, Murtaugh), I just hope they get their man. And from what it looks like, they're having one helluva time doing it. I just wish I could see how it all plays out.

I Interview Andrew McCarthy

Andrew McCarthy! I can't believe you're actually here! Please, have a seat.

Happy to be here, Mike. Nice place. What are all these things? Tissues?

Ah, no. Those are dryer sheets. I've been huffing them all morning in anticipation of your arrival. May I interest you in one? I have Tide, Bounce, Snuggle, Gain...

No, thank you, Mike. I'm fine.

Ok, your loss. I see that you're wearing some type of dress shoe. Are those Dockers?

They are, as a matter of fact. Good eye.

I can't help but wonder if maybe you would feel more comfortable in a pair of purple Converse sneakers like the ones you wore in Weekend at Bernie's.

What, seriously?

Yeah, kind of. I have a bunch of pairs in the other room if you want.

Why...why don't we start the interview? Does that sound okay?

Of course, of course. I'm sorry. Okay, first

question: What's going on with Weekend at Bernie's 3?

Um…there isn't going to be a Weekend…at Bernie's 3…

I find that hard to believe.

No, it's true, unfortunately. It's been over 20 years since the last one, and it wasn't well-received by audiences and I doubt it holds up too well over time.

I find it difficult to imagine what the audiences found so ludicrous about the second film.

Well, I think it's one thing to parade a dead guy around and string him up like some kind of marionette for a weekend like we did in the first one, but it's a whole 'nother thing when you're introducing voodoo and sunken treasure and having the corpse walk around whenever he hears music.

Seems like a natural plot progression to me.

I thought so too.

Because we all know it wasn't unfunny.

Yeah, it was a solid comedy, I thought.

Like that scene where Bernie is walking underwater….and-and-and-and-and- the harpoon….(laughing too hard to speak)

Yeah, it was pretty funny, wasn't it?

…right through his head!! Oh, my *goodness*, was that funny!

Yeah, yeah it was.

So, seriously, Andrew, what's the delay in W@B 3? Did Jonathon Silverman get signed on for

another season of *The Single Guy?*

The Single Guy? Mike, what year do you think we're—

I know he gets a lot of flack because he's got the most coveted time slot for any sitcom, right between Friends and Seinfeld, but I think it could stand on its own as a decent comedy.
Mike, you do know that I have done other things besides my work on the Bernie films, right?

I know that you were in *Mannequin.*

Yes, I was. I was.

Can you promise me that you will do *Weekend at Bernie's 3* before you do *Mannequin 3?* Mannequin 3? Mike, I wasn't even in the second one.

Just promise me, okay? It would break my heart if you did that.
Okay, fine. I promise not to do Mannequin 3 before I do Weekend at Bernie's 3.

Thank you.
Can we maybe talk about my other work, like the more recent stuff I am supposed to be promoting?

We could, I guess. But I am perusing my notes here and it seems that this interview is going to be heavy-handed with Bernie-related questions.
Well, what if I told you that I have done some other work; just in television alone for the past couple years I have been in Royal Pains, White Collar, Unforgettable, Lipstick Jungle...

Wow, really? I had no idea you did all those. And for each of those roles you had to carry around a corpse and pretend he was alive for a couple of days?

Come on, man…

Say, Andrew McCarthy, would you like to join my Weekend at Bernie's fan club? I've been trying to get another member besides myself for quite some time now and I think if I got you on as a card-carrying member, things will really pick up steam.

I don't really know, Mike…

…I take out ads in the paper with my phone number, I made a webpage, but all I get are harassing phone calls from people. All day long with the phone calls telling me to get a life…

Aw, I'm sorry to hear that, man. Well, maybe if you broadened the fan club instead of just relegating it to Weekend—

And they call me a "fag" and stuff…

…

…

…

Hey, Mike, my feet are kind of uncomfortable. Is it too late to ask for a pair of those purple Chucks?

Really? You're not just saying that, are you?

No, I mean it. I could really go for those sneakers.

Hot dog! Okay, great! I have some fishing line too in case you want to tie our limbs together and maybe you could drag me around the apartment or down to the bank...

Let's just start with the sneakers, okay, buddy?

You got it! Andrew McCarthy, everybody! Super nice guy!

As a Clairvoyant, I am Able to-- Hey, Where're You Going?

Hello, I can sense that there is something troubling you. It feels to me like there is a gaping hole in your family life. Did you lose someone close to you in the past few years? I can feel your sense of loss and I would like to tell you that everything is going to be okay. How do I know this? Well, it's simple: as a clairvoyant, I am able to--hey, where're you going?

What, you don't believe in clairvoyants? Let me tell you something: neither did I. At first. For too long I had shirked the notion that I had "the sight." I figured it was just allergies, but it wasn't. Not until I went to Medium School did I unlock the talents I held within myself. And now, with this degree of authenticity from Delphi University.com, I can speak to your recently deceased Mother...? No, wait--father? Brother? Close cousin?

I'm sorry, sometimes there is static interference. Is your cell phone on? Yeah, see, that's a problem. That was interfering with my sight, but that's okay. This is not a scam. Tarot cards are a scam. Any schmuck can pick up a pack of tarot cards and see into the future. Not everyone has $2275 to spend on a week- long seminar in which to hone their spiritual skills. Crystal balls are a scam too, obviously. They only cost a couple dollars at any thrift store. Any clairvoyant worth their salt knows that the more expensive their training is, the more it is sure to work.

Also notice how I refer to myself as a *clairvoyant* and not a *psychic.* The term "psychic" gets thrown around way too much these days and now it has lost all meaning. But if I call myself a *clairvoyant,* well, just listen to all those syllables! Why, it has just as many syllables as the word "scientist," so you know I am credible. While on the other hand, a "psychic" is nothing but a cheap imitator, relegated to back-alley store fronts and cheap tents at the carnival, whereas a clairvoyant will just walk up to any schmuck on the street and just start talking to them, much like what I am doing to you. See the difference? Do you remember that scene from *Pee-Wee's Big Adventure* with the gypsy woman and her crystal ball? See, that was a psychic. Case closed. So please, a little respect.

Let me be honest here. You have some dead

relatives standing next to you right now. Well, no, you can't see them; like I said earlier, I have the sight and you don't. No, you can't just start talking to them! That's not fair! You didn't get in correct alignment with your spirit guide to actualize the souls standing next to you. God, this is so frustrating! Let me put it this way: if you were possessed by evil spirits, would you trust the cobbler to get rid of them for you? No, of course not: you would trust your medieval barber to drill the holes in your head to let the demons fly out; not the cobbler. Now, allow me to channel the proper energies to get this message across to you.

Hey, please, just give me a second. This message is very important. It seems that your…grandmother…? Ha! Yes! Grandmother! Nailed it! It seems that your grandmother wants you… to… buy an… hour-long session with me to talk to her further. Come on, please? I have psychic--*clairvoyant* student loans to pay off.

The Unappreciated, Aspiring Author Files an Auto Insurance Claim

Describe the time of day and weather at the time of the accident:

The afternoon sunlight burst through my windshield with a Machiavellian magnificence, creating streaks of golden radiance that danced through my careening automobile.

Were you wearing a seatbelt at the time of the accident?

I remember tugging at the seatbelt with great fervor, convincing myself that it was strangling me in an attempt to keep me safe, when actually, 'twas I endangering the sanctity of the seatbelt with my thoughtless behavior.

In your own words, describe the cause of the accident:

Samantha said I loved the bottle; a bit too much at times. Often, when I would come home late and stinking drunk, she claimed I loved the bottle more than I loved her. Perhaps she was right. But a man in my line of work needs all of the numbing agents he can get his hands on. I remember saying to her one time, "Sam. Babe. Why you going all extreme on me? If you've seen some of the things I've seen, Toots, well, let me tell ya, you'd think twice about giving me a load of shit." Ah, Samantha, has it been that long since we last talked? Since we last touched?

Did you sustain any injuries because of the accident:
I remember looking at my shaking hands holding loosely onto the steering wheel. I focused on them as best I could and saw long, deep wrinkles, each one representing a trial or adverse scene in my life, each one more painful than the last. How many of these tests in life have I passed? More importantly, how many have I failed? The air bag had failed to deploy, causing a deep bruise on my forehead. It would heal in time. My pride, however, would not. Hell, I could have used another scar. Just tack on another failure. Oh, Samantha, where are you, babe?

If possible, name the other people involved in the accident:
Samantha and I used to picnic off of highway 341, taking the Gladstone exit and barreling up the hill on Brookview Road. From a distance, we would see our secluded spot; a grand oak tree that stood

in front of the entrance to a grove. As a child, my friends and I would venture out there on our Schwinn's and play Kick the Can until either dusk or when we fell over each other from youthful giddiness and innocence. Samantha and I carved our initials into that same tree years later, where the indentation of my '93 Saturn's fender now lays.

Comments welcome! Please leave this form in the break room or make copies and pass them out at random coffee houses or any place where you may find publishers. Thanks!

Insurance Agent's assessment/comments (office use only):

Claim denied.

This Vacuum Salesman Can't Believe Your Family Isn't Already Fucking Dead

Your Home, USA—Mark Rosen has just entered your home to show you the great suction and cleaning power of his new Shark Rocket cleaning system, and to be honest, he can't believe how you and your family have survived without it.

"Its suction power is better than that of the Dyson cleaning system, and at less cost," Mark exclaims as he pushes his way through your front door and into your life. "Once you see the Shark in action, you will wonder how you lived without it."

You can begin by telling Mark that you don't know what a Dyson cleaning system is, and that what he is plugging into your wall looks a heck of a lot like a vacuum cleaner.

"It's not *just* a vacuum cleaner," Mark explains while pushing his glasses back up to his face, slightly out of breath from excitement. "It's a system of cleaning that will render you breathless. Watch!"

Mark then lays out a fine line of dirt all over

your carpet and asks you if you have any children. And if you do have children, he wants to know if they play outside frequently. You tell Mark that you are not comfortable giving a vacuum cleaner salesman that kind of information and he apologizes, but not by first telling you that children carry all sorts of dirt and germs from outside the home *into* the home, and without a proper system of cleaning, a la a Shark Rocket, your children will be susceptible to asthma and airborne allergens that can render your children helpless.

Mark turns the vacuum cleaner on and sucks up the line of dirt while saying, "Your home is where your family should feel safest, but how can they be if it makes them sick?"

Before you can tell Mark to get the hell out of your goddamn house, he turns the vacuum off and unhinges the vacuum's collection box to show you all the filth and dirt that are hiding in your carpet. "Do you see all of this," he asks in amazement. "Your fragile children have been breathing this in for goodness knows how long!"

You begin to feel like you have failed your family, because well, you have. Without the Shark Rocket, your family is not safe from their own home. It is your job and responsibility as a parent for your children's well-being and you can't even do that. Christ, if you had only known. This is the kind of stuff they don't teach in college.

Mark can see in your eyes the desperation and despair. "It's okay," Mark says calmly and assuredly. "It's going to be okay. You didn't know. But now you can do something about it. For just five payments of $39.99, you can keep your family safe from your ignorance."

You begin to get your checkbook, but first begin to wonder how human beings have been able to survive this long without the assistance of the Shark Rocket. After all, it's only been around for a couple of years and already we have a world that is overpopulated. Perhaps it was wrong of you to assume that the Shark Rocket vacuum system was on par with penicillin or the cure for Polio. Maybe you should go back to the living room and tell Mark to fuck off.

Uh-oh. Is he holding some billiard balls? Is he preparing to further display the incredible suction power of the Shark Rocket? Okay, if that Shark Rocket cleaning system really can suck in all those billiard balls, I think he may have a valid point about your child's health. But maybe you want to get that old bowling ball out of the closet first. After all, you can't be too sure of these things.

Advice Column: Ask Charles Bukowski

Dear Mr. Bukowski,
I've been married to my husband for almost 15 years
now. I love my hubby to death, but I just wish he was a
little bit more romantic at times. We have a vacation full
of apple-picking and antiquing in the fall and I would
love to spice things up in the bedroom by then. What am
I going to do?
Signed,
Worried in Warrington.

You will eat, sleep, fuck, piss, shit, clothe yourself,
walk around and bitch.

Dear Chuck,
I've been stuck in the same assistant manager position
for quite some time now, but I am too shy to ask for a
raise. I was hoping that my work ethic alone would get
me the bump I deserve, but now I see that I need to
mention it to them myself. How do I get the confidence to
approach my boss about the subject?
Signed,
Fearful in Frankford.

Meyers had once controlled the American Clock
Company but drinking and a bad marriage had
ruined him. He had to sell most of his stock and
was now only an assistant manager. He had gone

*on the wagon and as a result was always irritable.
Meyers was continually trying to draw Frank out
and make him angry. Then he would have an
excuse to fire him. There was nothing worse than
a reformed drunk and a Born Again Christian and
Meyers was both...*

**Dear Charlie,
You got to help me. I think my gambling is beginning to
spiral out of control. I've been staying out too late,
completely losing my sense of time when I'm placing
bets. Heck, I even missed my son's 8th birthday party
because I was trying to rouse up some quick cash because
I was falling behind and needed to recoup my previous
losses. How do I break this bedeviling cycle?
--Desperate in Des Moines**

*"...in the next race the four horse figures best and
they are giving six-to-one odds..."*

*Victoria let out a sexy, "Oooh...?" She leaned over
to look at his program, touching him with her
arm. Then he felt her leg press against his.
"People just don't know how to rate a horse," he
told her. "Show me a man who can rate a horse
and I'll show you a man who can win all the
money he can carry."*

**Hey, Chazzy B!
I'm super-excited to sign my son up for his first season of
summer baseball! I loved playing the game when I was a**

kid, even though my own father was terribly critical and
competitive and I do not want to repeat that same kind of
harsh criticism onto my kid. Is there a way to allow my
son to have fun while also learning and cultivating the
competitive instincts one needs in order to be a well-
rounded individual?

--Hesistant in Hastings

*I raised the Jimmy Foxx Slugger, came down with
it and caught him squarely on top of the head. He
didn't drop. He just stood there staring at me. I hit
him again. It was like an old time comedy movie
in black and white. He just stood there and made
a horrible face at me. I slipped out from behind
the garbage cans and started to walk away. He
followed me.*

*I turned around. "Leave me alone," I told him.
"Let's forget it."*

Another Slow Day at the Suicide Prevention Center

Hey, guys, thanks for having this quick meeting in the conference room. I just have a few things to say and then we can get back out there. Alright, first thing, Gary, you're hoarding all the donuts. They're good donuts, I know, that's why I brought them for everybody; so we call all enjoy them, not just you. Secondly, we might all lose our jobs in a week.

OK, there was a better way to phrase that, I know. It's just...it's really quiet out there, ok? Like, super- duper quiet. Like, where my thoughts actually seem to create noise; that is how quiet it is out there. Which is good. It's a *good* thing. I am not saying that people living with purpose is a bad thing, but...damn, I mean, doesn't anyone want to commit suicide anymore?

I remember the good old days when some poor person would (looks directly at Gary) *get called fat and ugly*, then they'd swallow a bunch of pills and give us a call. Whatever happened to that?

Now all I hear is Gary's heavy breathing from across the room. I don't see how we can get public funding if we all sit around and listen to Gary getting fatter. When PBS does their fundraiser, do they show some middle-aged, overweight tub of shit eating a box of donuts? No! They play their strongest, most well-liked programs, like, *Downton Abbey* or that one where the guy lives in the woods for 50 years. What's it called? *Alone in the Forest?* Whatever.

Look, here's what I know: we are good at preventing suicides. We just need people to call. So please, if you know of anyone that just looks pathetic or is living some sort of delusion that their life actually has *purpose* or-or-or-or-or-*meaning*...please, tell them the truth, then give them our number.

Giving them our number is important to this whole process. I can't stress that enough. You want to give a person a gun, not the bullets. No, wait. We're not the gun in this metaphor. We're the safety. Then who's the bullets? Society? Oh, fuck it.

Hey, Gary, listen. I am sorry for harshing on you during this meeting; you're just as unattractive as you are large. Gary, how is your home life going? Everything going well? How is Stacey? Good. Did...did you know I saw her coming out of the White Castle burger joint last week? Yeah, she was with some guy, I don't know, it's really none of my business.

Hey, didn't you once tell me that she was your whole world? Your reason for living? Just curious. Alright, let's go back out there. Gary, if you want to knock off early you go right ahead. You have your cell phone on you? Got our number at the ready? Ok, great. Alright, good meeting, guys. Let's get back out there and save some lives!

The Ultimate Way

Thank you, sir, for seeing me on such short notice. I cannot imagine how busy you must be. And you're probably wondering, "Who is this Jenkins fellow? From what department?" But I am sure your most daunting question most likely revolves around my face-paint.

Well, Sir, my name is Michael Jenkins. I have been working with your company for over four years. I manage the Accounts Receiving Department, and this face-paint that I am wearing is modeled after WWE superstar "The Ultimate Warrior."

And I want a raise.

Mr. Pensky, as I am sure you know, Accounts Receiving has shown a steady 3.6 percent increase per year since I have taken over the department and, besides the great satisfaction it gives me to contribute so much to the company, I have not received any kind of incentive for the effort.

Hey, did you know that when the Ultimate Warrior beat Hulk Hogan at Wrestlemania IV, it was the first time the Hulkster lost by pinfall at a Pay-Per-View event? It's true.

Despite the face-paint, Mr. Pensky, the Ultimate Warrior does not clown around and neither do I. Sure, my office-mates and underlings chuckled a bit upon seeing my appearance, but now, after seeing the results I bring in, they chuckle with *respect.*

Do you respect me, Mr. Pensky? You should. The numbers don't lie. Why do you think I look like *this?* I'm out there every day, hunting down leads, slaying customer dissatisfaction, trouncing delinquent payments, making the sea run red with our rival's stocks.

Please stop staring at my boot tassels, sir. Eyes up here.

I mean, who do you think got the Merrymead account? Let me assure you, I wouldn't have gotten it that day if I were dressed as Andre the Giant, A.K.A, *The Gentle Giant.*

Sure, I could have decorated myself in the garb of Randy "Macho Man" Savage, but it would have fallen flat. Trust me, I've tried that before. And who else would fit so perfectly as the Ultimate Warrior when asking for a raise? Ric Flair? Brutus "The Barber" Beefcake? How about Bret "The

Hitman" Hart, A.K.A. *The Excellence of Execution?* Actually, that last one doesn't sound half bad: The Excellence of Execution. Damn, that would have been kind of catchy for this meeting. Oh, well. Can't go back now. The Warrior is in.

Hmmmm...well, hell, there's also "Mr. Wonderful" Paul Orndorff. That would have been pretty smooth...George "The Animal" Steele..."Ravishing" Rick Rude...

Mr. Pensky, maybe we should hold off on this meeting. Maybe schedule it for another time. I have to prepare a better argument. "Million Dollar Man" Ted Dibiase! Dammit! Mr. Pensky, I'm sorry, I have to go! I will reschedule with your secretary.

I Believe This Book You Lent Me Has Spent Some Considerable Time in Your Bathroom

Citing it as, "the book that genuinely defines our generation," you placed this paperback in my hands and told me that I would be remiss if I didn't scan these pages; these frayed, peeled-back pages.

That should have been the first clue that I was handling something soaked in your own waste: the frayed pages. The upper right corner especially was peeled back and aged something awful, despite the fact that the book was published nary a year ago. And the cover—my god, the cover was peeled back so far I couldn't even make out the title. Optimistically, I thought it might have been due to frequent usage. "He sure does like opening this book," I hoped.

But the further I went along with my reading, the less I could ignore the telltale signs, starting with the prematurely-aged pages. They could only be produced in an environment of rapid moisture and quick evaporation. Last I checked, we do not live in Canberra. But do you know what weather system is similar to that of the Australian coastline? That's right—your shitter.

My theory was only strengthened when I analyzed some stained liquid droplets starting with the title page. They are much too defined and disheartening to be from a wisp of water vapor; no, no, no. Water evaporates. Water that is laced with ammonia stains. These pages are stained.

Our friendship is stained.

I didn't want to believe it. "I've known him for years," I thought. "Why would he do this to me?" And then I opened up to page 45 and saw the pubic hair. How I wished it was only an eyelash, then lo and behold only 10 pages later I came across my first tuft of wiry hairs. The first of many tufts in my journey to the end of this novel. T'were I to discover said tuft in my lobster tail, I would promptly return it; no if's, and's, or but's!

All complaints aside, looking at all these tufts, you should seriously see someone about that.

Do you remember what you said to me? You said, "This is the best book I ever read." Do you remember that? You looked me dead in the eye and said that. Best book you ever read? Sadly, no. First off, weak plot, unsympathetic characters, and piss droplets. What books have you been reading? I would hazard a guess and assume that most of your library at home consists of Dr. Seuss books and various adventures of Babar.

Gah, to think of all the times I held that book and then itched my eye!

Oh, and another thing: "Defines our generation"? What are you saying about our generation? That we're constipated? Constipated for change? Please shut up. The next time I see you, I will recommend a book to you and promptly shove your head in my toilet.

Catalogue Writer's Block

Stop the presses! We can't go to print! Andy, hit the pause button there, thanks. This latest issue is missing an article. No, not for the Himalayan Walking Shoes; it was a little late, but it was a hell of a thought-provoking article. Good job, Benes. What we are missing here is the description for the Comfort Wipe. You know, that thing you use in the bathroom... you put toilet paper on one end and wipe... yeah, the Shit Stick. I'm missing the description for the Shit Stick. Where is it??

Do any of you maggots realize the stress running this catalogue brings me? I assure, you do not, for you are not a rotund old man who feverishly gnaws on unlit cigars and chances are you're not wearing this fancy badge my wife made me when I got this promotion.

Guys, I'm not saying that your jobs are easy. I'm sorry if I am flying off the handle like this, and even though we are regarded as junk mail that just turns up in your mailbox at random, we still have deadlines, people!

Now, where is the Comfort Wipe description? Well, if you have it, give it here. Alright, let me just give this a quick once-over…

…

…

Dammit, Jenkins. Stand right there. Ok, everyone, listen up! I want you to hear this. The incomparable Mr. Jenkins here has written us a *perfect* example on how to *not* write a good catalogue product description.

(Ahem) "Tired of endlessly reaching behind you for sanitary purposes? Maybe you are unable to reach your rear because you are overweight or were cursed with T-Rex arms. Perhaps you resemble more a dwarf than an actual human being…"

Is something funny, Jenkins? Tell me, what name is on the side of this building that you are standing in at this moment? Is it, "Hammacher Schlemmer"? No. What is it, then? That's right: Harriet goddamn Carter. Distinctive Goddamn Gifts Since Nineteen-Fifty-Fuckin'-Eight!

Yeah, I know you lost your hermit crab, and I'm sorry about that. I let you keep those framed pictures of his shell all around your office, didn't I? He was camera shy. I get it. But he died like, two months ago! So if you bring up your deceased hermit crab any more as an excuse as to why you can't do your job, I want you to find a quiet place and concentrate really hard, and maybe, if you close your eyes tight and focus, you might actually hear me not giving a shit.

This job has given me an ulcer, Jenkins, and you are the reason why I am out of Pepto.

Listen here: I'm giving you one more chance, and then, if you can't give me a decent description, I'm going to show you the door. That's a promise. I've seen this business chew up and spit out the most talented product description writers that this world has never even gotten to know. Hell, if Sharper Image were around at the time, Hemingway's lights would have gone out well before The Sun Also Rises.

Now, pay attention: here is your last chance, kiddo. For the fall catalogue, if you can't write me an invoking, I-need-this-item-or-I-will-surely-die product description, you're finished. Washed up. No catalogue will ever touch you when I am done with you. Not even the Burpee Seed Catalogue will look at you. By next Friday, I want a beautiful, poetic, lyrical description of item number 3322: Rubber Bed Sheets. Available in all sizes, from Twin to King. Can you do that, or are you going to go over to your desk and type me up your resignation? The choice is yours.

What I'd Say to my Crewmates if I were In Cortez's Army and He Just Purposely Sank Our Ships

(Watching the final ship burn and sink to the sea floor)

...

...

...

Okay, that may have been the most fucked up thing I've ever seen. I'm sorry, I'm having trouble believing it. Renaldo, did I just see that? Did I just see him burn our ships? What's more, did I see all you assholes cheer when he did it? I must be tripping. I hate to be the bearer of bad news here, but you do know that we travel by boat in order to get back to our homes and families, right? And now that bearded devil sank our boats. Now, I'm no mathematician, but it looks like, hold on... let me do a quick count here... yep. We are left with zero boats. We now have no boats and last I checked, boats are what keep us from getting royally screwed in a strange, antagonistic land. Ergo, we're fucked!

Well, big apologies over here if I'm sounding a little panicky! It's kind of a big deal when you have no means of transportation and you're living in a land where everybody wants to kill you. I don't care if it was a good speech; he burned our boats! Yeah, maybe if I had been listening to Mr. Cortez's speech, you're right, but I have A.D.D. This is not news, as I've told you this before many times, Hidalgo.

Maybe he did say some truly inspiring things before he stranded us here in this hostile land full of tan people and war paint and spears and lances and... what's the name of the sword these people use? It's got sharpened flint or volcanic stone on the sides...Maqua-something. One time I saw an Aztec take a horse's head clean off with one swipe of it. It's true! The whole damn head! Maquahuitl? Is that what it's called? Whatever. I'll be sure to politely ask the next Aztec the proper pronunciation before he uses it to chop my goddamn soul apart.

Oh, my god, we're so fucked.

Why would he do this? How was this ever a good idea to him? At what point was he like, "You know what I hate? Contingencies. Boy, I hate the idea of a safe retreat back home in case one of like, a billion- jillion things goes wrong."

How is this good leadership?

What if they have mega-lions here? Has anyone thought of that? Lions that can swallow you whole. Or if the Aztecs are host to some exotic parasite that latches onto your pancreas and makes you shit out your mouth or something? What, you've never heard of mega-lions? Of course you haven't because that's why you cheered when our boats sank. You cheered because you aren't thinking of the unimaginable.

Personally, between you, me, and the wall here, I am not too fond of being shat out of a giant lion's ass or shitting out of my own mouth, respectively. But that's just me! That's just me and I'm sure I'm in the minority with that opinion. It's just...it would have been nice to ask us first. If he just sidled up next to us and was casually like, "Hey, bro. Random question: if our boats were to suddenly, I don't know, *disappear*, would you be more motivated to overthrow the Aztec Empire, less motivated, or indifferent to taking over the Aztec Empire? Just curious." You know, something like that. And we would have given him feedback. I'm just saying a vote would have been nice.

I would have voted to keeping the boats seaworthy, I don't know about you guys.

It's insecurity is what it is. Everything has to be so over-the-top with him that with every decision he has to go big or go home. Sorry, poor choice of words. None of us are going home; not anymore. All he had to do was just ask us sincerely if we could overtake this empire for him, that's all. We would have done it gladly! He didn't have to make some big extravagant scene and strand us here to die. That's the mark of an insecure leader, no lie. But don't tell him I said that, ok?

And what was that whole part of his speech about Jesus Christ? Did he seriously bring up Jesus Christ during his speech? God, what balls. What balls on this fucking guy. Yeah, we have Jesus Christ, who is just one guy, but did you ever think that maybe these Aztecs have like, a hundred gods? Well, they do, Antonio. And one of them is a flying snake! A goddamn snake with feathers! Who comes up with this shit? Honestly. A giant, feathered snake with a conch shell around its neck! And that's one of the more pedestrian gods. No, of course, you're right. We have the scrawny guy hung up on a couple pieces of wood. He'll help us win; of course he will. Don't worry, everyone! Our *pacifist god* will help us win this *war!*

Did he ever think of *our* options? You know, we don't *have* to stay. Didn't he realize that we are in a completely unexplored land? We have no idea how far it goes, what kind of riches it contains, whether it be animals or vegetation or other natural resources. I could easily just wander off in any direction I choose. And you know me, I'm personable! I'd get along just fine with my dashing good looks and rapier wit if I came across any natives. So what if I'm pale-skinned? I'll just tell them I have Vitiligo. Boom. Done. Or I'd just walk and walk and walk until I fell off the Earth.

Man, there are days and there are days...!

Well, yeah, I mean, I'll fight. I'll definitely fight. I didn't say I wasn't going to fight, I just wanted to get that off my chest first. Yes, let's overtake this land in the name of Jesus Christ. Hot dog, I'm motivated! Boy, I hope these Aztecs can build us some ships when this is all over.

Aw, Man! Rudy Found a Dumpster Baby

Hey, guys! Have you heard? Rudy found a dumpster baby! No joke! Haven't you been watching the news? You been hiding under a rock or something? It was all over the news last week. Rudy was moseying along Second Street Tuesday morning, doing his usual dumpster diving, and he heard the cries of a hungry baby.

Crazy, right?

I don't know who would throw away a perfectly good baby. They're still trying to find the parents. Can you imagine how heartless you would have to be abandon your infant child? Isn't that terrible? I don't know what's going to happen to the baby; maybe they find the parents and have them arrested and the grandparents become the legal guardians, I don't know how it works exactly. But without speculating too much, I can safely say that the real victims of this ordeal are going to be us: the friends of Rudy.

Remember how much shit we used to give him for rooting through other people's trash? Ever since we were kids and we'd walk home from school, he couldn't resist a quick rummaging of the trash. It was like, "Dude, both your parents have jobs. You live in a house. What the hell are you trash-picking for?"

And he always replied, "Hey, you never know." As if that could excuse any behavior relegated to street urchins.

Street urchins, orphans, bums... whatever, Tom. Get off my back.

Well, this dumpster-baby business has just reaffirmed all those years of trash picking for Rudy. It's like the Powerball of trash-finds. And we are never going to hear the end of it. Remember when he found those cufflinks on the men's room floor of the movie theater? Do you remember how bad that was? He just went on and on and on about the cufflinks. Did it even matter that he doesn't own a suit? Fuck no! Because it wasn't about the fashion, right? It was about *finding* something. And it's all he talked about for weeks. Well, that was nothing, okay? That was *nothing* compared to how bad he is now that he's found a baby in the trash.

I was hanging out with him yesterday. We

were walking to the coffee shop and he's spouting all these statistics about infanticide, teen pregnancy... all this shit. And you know what he says? He says, "I just feel so powerless knowing that I can't save them all."

Can you believe that? Can you believe he *said* that? Oh, and by the way, while we're walking to the place, he's stopping at every. Single. Trash can. "Just making sure," he says, "Just making sure." God, you find one crying baby in the trash can and suddenly you're Jesus Christ.

Do you have any idea how many babies are discarded in public places every year? I do. Why do I know that? I shouldn't know that!

If the baby was dead, I totally would have patted Rudy on the back because that's a tough find. Dead babies don't make noise. But this baby was crying. There were sounds emanating from the trash can. Any one of us would have done the same thing. It just so happened that Rudy is a lifelong dumpster diver, so now all of his years of trash-picking has been endorsed.

So, if you're going to be hanging out with Rudy any time soon, I'm just giving you a heads up. No, Tony, I don't know if you should "congratulate" him. Do you congratulate someone for finding an abandoned child? Maybe you could say, "Good job on performing your civic duty," something formal like that. Personally, I would just avoid the guy for a couple years altogether.

How DOMINO'S 2 for 1 Medium Pizza Deal (limit one topping) Saved My Marriage

My wife and I: we lead busy lives. Like most modern families, we are a two-income household, so you can imagine how stressful our days can be. I am some kind of middle-management something or other and my wife, she um, well, she wears a lady-suit. Gray, usually. With small shoulder pads.

We hustle and bustle through our workday, putting out fires and stuff, so when we both get home after handling all sorts of stressful workday stuff, *then* deciding who is going to make what for dinner? Well, why don't you just give us each a loaded gun? That's how dangerous it is.

The weekday dinner is where everything that is wrong in our marriage comes to a head. The mutual stresses of both our days coalesce as we decide what to do to feed ourselves. My wife and I, we come home at the same time and the house is in a whirlwind of chaos. Both our children, 14 year old Cody and 12 year old Skylar have been running rampant throughout the house, lampshades crooked, shedding uneven light on the living room, our family portraits hanging askew on the walls. Cody goes cruising about the house on his skateboard sipping on a juice box while Skylar jumps rope around the dining room table, knocking over various knick-knacks that my wife collected during our many weekends spent thrift shopping in various cozy towns.

My wife and I, while all this is going on, we're supposed to not only corral our children, but also supply dinner? Are you crazy?

So, while all this is going on, we just scream at each other back and forth. "Well, what about spaghetti??" one of us would shout at one end of the kitchen.

"Spaghetti?" the other would shout back. "You impotent ass! How can we be expected to make spaghetti?? Spaghetti? Where do you even start with that??"

And so on and so forth.

Usually what ends up happening is that by 7:00 we are holding each other in the middle of the kitchen just crying our eyes out. The family and I go to sleep unfed. That's most nights.

But now, thanks to DOMINO'S 2 for 1 Medium Pizza Deal (limit one topping)... Wait, hold on, I'm getting ahead of myself.

Cody was hit by a bus.

It wasn't something that we were planning on, nor were we expecting it to be the greatest thing to ever happen to our marriage. My wife and I were doing our usual thing about dinner (I think our argument was about fish sticks, not spaghetti), and Cody did his usual thing, streaming through the kitchen on his skateboard, sipping on a juice-box. We could have told him to stop and sit down, but we didn't.

You can't stop Cody. He's a free spirit and we are proud of him for that.

So a moment after Cody cruised through the kitchen we heard a loud screech of an automobile's brakes followed by a wet smack.

Cody got creamed.

Later, in the hospital, the doctor was telling us that a coma can last anywhere from a day to several years.

We spent many nights in that hospital, waiting, hoping. My wife refused to speak with me, citing that if I had simply made dinner and not put up an argument with her, Cody would have been sitting on the dining room table eating a hastily prepared meal instead of lying like a mangled heap in a hospital bed.

I couldn't argue with her. I'm a modern man unable to feed my family.

Until that is...

One Wednesday night, two weeks into Cody's free-spirited coma, I arrived in the hospital room holding two medium DOMINO'S pizzas. The setting sun casted a beautiful orange light on the blue and red boxes of pizzas, the grease spots, like a teenager's face, created a beautifully sexy sheen. My wife looked at me longingly as I held my bounteous feast.

"What—whatcha got there?" she asked, letting go of Cody's limp hand and walking towards me.

"I have two medium DOMINO'S pizzas."

"Two," she asked me. Her voice about to raise, ready for an argument.

"I saw an advertisement on television," I told her. "Their C.E.O., Patrick Doyle, said that it's still tough out there financially, and that people are in need of a good deal, so he is offering a medium pizza two for one deal (limit one topping) on Wednesdays after 4:00 p.m."

She leaned in close and whispered, "Patrick Doyle. Can you trust him?"

I whispered back in her ear, "I trust him more than I trust myself. How would you like a slice of DOMINO'S pizza?" I barely got the second sentence out before we started kissing. Our passion was so overwhelming, we made love right there on the hospital room floor. I think I heard Skylar's jump rope hit the floor, but I can't be sure. Like I said, it was a transcending meal/love-making session.

We used to have a strained marriage, but now, thanks to DOMINO'S 2 for 1 medium pizza deal (limit one topping), we can now feel assured in the fact that even with our busy lives, we can still provide for our family.

Cody is still touch and go or something.

I Interview Jim Rome

Jim Rome! Thank you so much for making it out here today!

Thank you for having me, Mike. Nice place you have here.

Thank you. And thank you for dressing up; you look sleek.

Oh, that's how I usually dress. I see you got some jam-jams on. What kind of sequins are those on your pants? Polar bears?

They're my power animal, Jim. I will not apologize for that.

Fair enough.

I gotta say, I am digging on the goatee you got growing there. Most movies and television shows, if there is an evil doppleganger going around, he's got a goatee. That's how they differentiate him from the main character.

Yeah…?

What I mean is, is there a good version of you out there somewhere?

Are you serious?

No, I'm kidding of course; just a little banter before we get started. Now, Jim, for those of us out there who have no idea who you are, who are you?

I am a sports talk show host.

Yes, you have quite a few shows out there where you talk about sports. Sports are fun.

And they're fun to talk about too! People love to hear my opinions on the latest sports headlines.

Ok, so to quickly recap your role in society: you offer your opinions on sports news. Now, an opinion is a personal belief based not on certainty. And a sport is a game or recreational activity.

Yes, I believe so.

And you get paid for this?

Yes. Quite handsomely, I might add.

I love this country.

Pardon me?

I'm just sayin'. America, ya know? Fuck yeah.

Yes yes.

And I see that one of the posters for your show *Rome is Burning* is you holding a microphone that looks like a gun. May I ask why?

The tagline reads, "Anything is open game," meaning that I will tackle any issue and profess my opinion on it. And sometimes my opinions can be offensive to some people.

When you host that show, do you have a gun under your chin as if it were a microphone?

(sighs) No, Mike. I do not.

That's a shame. I would pay for cable to see that. Now, the title, *Rome is Burning*, that's a fanciful

pun on your last name. Do you say the same thing when you have a fever?

What?

Or, say when you have a prostate exam, and the doctor sticks his finger up there, does he say something clever like, "When in Rome..."
Is there a reason why I am here? What's with this interview?

Yeah, it's falling off the rails a bit, isn't it? I have more puns, though. But I'll try to be professional. Ok, let's get back to it. Were you a former professional sports player before getting on the T.v?
No, no I was not. I was into broadcasting mostly: the coverage of sports.

Well, you know what they say: "Those who can, do. Those who can't, teach." But you're not really teaching, either. We need to amend that saying for you, Jim. I'll work on it.
Thank you.

How about: "Those who can, do. Those who can't, teach. Those who can do neither, criticize."
And those who can't criticize wear polar bear pajamas.

You cut deep, Jim. How are you still even here?
I have the 21st most listened to radio show in the *country*, understand? I am touted as one of the biggest opinion makers in my generation.

We're not the same generation are we?

No, I don't believe so.

Whew! I'm sorry, you were saying…?
I was saying that being as famous as I already am, it takes a lot of work to get new listeners.

Oh, shit. Wait, Jim. I think there is some mistake. I, uh…I don't have much *pull*, readership-wise. In fact, I was using your name to get some new readers myself.

You're kidding.

No, sadly, I am not. Now, please…don't…don't get upset and flip the table over. It's particle-board.
I'm leaving. Scratch that—I'm *out!*

Jim, thanks for being a good…sport.
Go to hell, you pathetic media trilobite.

Jim Rome, everybody!

I'm Sure Mathew Broderick Still Sometimes Feels Bad About Those Two People He Ran Over in 1987

Hey, we've all done some rude things. Why, just last week I saw someone sneeze and I didn't say, "Gesundheit." Rude, right? But it's okay because I totally felt bad about it after the moment passed to say it, and that was over 6 days ago! And in that same remorseful vein, I'm sure Matthew Broderick still sometimes feels bad about those two people he killed with his car in Ireland back in 1987.

Now, you aren't really living unless you've wronged some people, and it just so happens that Matthew Broderick was living life to the fullest when he was driving his red BMW through a few sloped roads and souls of the small Irish town of…what's it called? Enniskillen? Seriously? Ennis-*kill*en? As if Mathew probably sometimes didn't feel bad enough, thanks. Thanks a lot!

Granted, the two people whose lives he ended were not celebrities. In fact, they were Irish peasants, but people none the same, I'm told! And it really shows how down to earth and approachable Matthew Broderick is even though he had just starred in the movie that would make him a legend: *Ferris Bueller's Day Off*, just don't approach him while he is in his car, even if he is driving on the wrong side of the road at speed.

Why, I wouldn't be surprised if Matthew offered the family of the victims an autograph or two to show that there were no hard feelings, even though he did suffer a broken leg for his troubles. A broken leg that he did not deserve, mind you, but still, he probably didn't complain too much about it. I guess he would just have to wait six weeks before jumping and hopping through people's living rooms and backyards in order to get home on time.

And speaking of *Ferris Bueller's Day Off*, do you know who was in the car with Matthew at the time of the incident? Actress Jennifer Gray! Talk about an 80's power couple! They aren't together anymore, but I wonder if she ever calls Matthew to reminisce about old times and as they laugh about some funny things that happened on the set of the movie, Jennifer might refer to the accident that killed two people (they probably call it something vague and cool like, "The Incident") and she'd say something like, "God, wasn't that so messed up when that happened?"

And Matthew is probably like, "Yeah. Yeah, it was."

I also wonder what the victims thought of the whole thing right before they died. If they were just regular people like you and me, I'm sure the last thing the woman said as blood trickled out of her ear was, "Wow, is that Matthew Broderick?" Because that's what I would say. It'd be a real shame if they died on impact, not realizing they had just met the young and charismatic star.

It was probably unimaginably difficult for Mathew to go back to acting after that. It wouldn't surprise me if he tried to inject some of the Irish Incident into each of his movie roles thereafter. He probably offered David Kellogg a little more character depth for one of his movies. "David," he probably said, "What if---and I'm just spit-balling here, but what if Inspector Gadget was let go with a smack on the wrist after running over a couple of Europeans? And we can just see where the character goes from there."

Go-go Gadget turpitude!

I'm sure he still sometimes feels bad about it. Especially if he comes across some internet meme or factoid about the '87 events. It might deflate his self-esteem and force him to sit on his balcony overlooking the beach and rethink his life; good decisions and bad. After a short while, his movie star wife might see the long look on his face and offer some consolation from his mental fatigue, stating that it was an accident and that nothing could be done. With just small kiss from her tender lips, his guilt will recede and he'll go, "You're right, Sara Jessica Parker. You're right. Come on, let's go to the premier."

Setting the Doomsday Clock

Characters:

Dr. Rumack—Leader of the Legion of Doom. Tries to steer **Dr. Lewis** in the ways of the clock-setting.

Dr. Blair---Over-emotional doctor, eager to set the clock according to his specifications

Dr. Kelly—Quiet member of the legion. Does not say much, except when needed to cause a commotion.

Dr. Lewis—Newest member of the Legion. Asking

thought-provoking questions and wonders why

there needs to be a doomsday clock at all, much to

Dr. Rumack's disappointment

Dr. Rumack: Dr. Lewis! Come in! Come in! I'm so glad you could make it.

Dr. Lewis: Thank you, Dr. Rumack. It's an honor

to work with you! I've been looking forward to this for quite some time!

Dr. Rumack: Mmm, yes. Let me introduce you to the rest of the group here. This is Dr. Blair

Dr. Blair: Hello.

Dr. Rumack: …And Dr. Kelly

Dr. Kelly: Hello, Dr. Lewis, welcome aboard.

Dr. Lewis: Thank you. Thank you so much! I think we are going to do some great work together.

Dr. Rumack: I'm sorry that we do not have a uniform for you just yet, but your addition to the club has been very last minute

Dr. Lewis: Oh, please don't apologize, it's quite alright…

Dr. Kelly: We're called the Legion of Doom!

Dr. Rumack: Yes, Dr. Kelly, that's what we call ourselves.

Dr. Kelly: See? It's like the Superman costume, but with a big D instead of an S, and it's like a lab-coat for a cape…

Dr. Rumack: Okay, Dr. Kelly, why don't you take it down a notch, okay? We have work to do.

Dr. Lewis: It's clever. I like that. But don't worry about the uniform; I'm sure it will get taken care of.

Dr. Rumack: Right! So! Onward to work! First order of business, I think, should be a re-evaluation of the Doomsday Clock setting.

Dr. Kelly & Dr. Blair: Yes yes!

Dr. Rumack: Right now it is set at 5 minutes to midnight, but I think we can get it a little closer than that. After all, we do have environmental concerns to deal with now as well as nuclear annihilation. Dr. Blair!

Dr. Blair: Yes, Dr. Rumack!

Dr. Rumack: What new information do you have regarding environmental hazards?

Dr. Blair: Well, last week, I saw my neighbor put his used double A batteries in the regular trash bin. And on my way here this morning, I saw some guy driving a diesel car without a gas cap!

Dr. Rumack: Oh, my! Were you able to find out how long he had been driving and where he was going?

Dr. Blair: Yes, fortunately I was able to pull up next to him and get...

Dr. Lewis: I'm sorry to interrupt, but what are you talking about, Dr. Blair?

Dr. Blair: I'm talking about threats to humanity, obviously.

Dr. Rumack: Continue, please, Dr. Blair. Were you able to find out how much he had been driving today?

Dr. Blair: Yes, well, first I threatened him that I would move the Doomsday Clock up for what I had seen, but he wasn't taking me seriously…

Dr. Lewis: Excuse me, maybe I'm speaking out of place, but it sounds like you're just pointing stuff out that you saw on the way here.

Dr. Blair: That's ludicrous. I'm talking about everyday environmental hazards that will cause the world to end, that's all. And from what I've seen today, scientifically, I think we can safely move the clock to 11:58.

Dr. Lewis: Don't you think that will cause a panic?

Dr. Blair: That guy in the Humvee needs to know that he is choking the world.

Dr. Kelly: I once saw a kid using one of those spray cans to write his name on the wall of some building. It was like, CHSSSSSSSSSSSSSSSSSSS!

Dr. Blair: Oh, 11:58 for sure. Maybe even 11:59.

Dr. Lewis: Whoa, hold on here a second. You guys can't be serious.

Dr. Rumack. Dr. Lewis, just be cool about this, okay? We're scientists, man. I think we know how to gather data and form it into usable information.

Dr. Lewis: But it sounds like they just want to cause a panic.

Dr. Rumack: Certainly not! Why, don't you remember when the Soviet Union fell and the Berlin Wall came down? We set the clock aaaaaaaaaalllllll the way back to 11:43. You remember that?

Dr. Lewis: Yeah, about that....what if the Soviet Union won the Cold War and democracy fell? Would you still put it at 11:43?

Dr. Rumack: Of course not! We'd put it at midnight, for sure! Or Quarter after.

Dr. Lewis: But if the whole point was that two nations aren't pointing nuclear missiles at each other anymore, then it doesn't matter who wins, so long as they're not doing it anymore, right?

Dr. Rumack: Yeah, but the communists are evil. That goes without saying.

Dr. Lewis: Isn't what you call "evil" nothing but a relative term? What if the Soviet Union had a doomsday clock in Moscow? What would they set the clock to in 1989?

Dr. Rumack: There's another Doomsday clock team? What do they call themselves? The Watch Men?

Dr. Blair: Second(s) Story?

Dr. Kelly: Power Hour?

Dr. Rumack: Minute Men!

Dr. Blair and **Dr. Kelly:** (agreeing happily with Dr. Rumack's choice)

Dr. Lewis: I just don't see where Science can try to quantify exactly how fucked we are as a species with a clock. 11:58. 11:57. What the hell does that mean, anyway?

Dr. Blair: It means that jerk in the Hummer better not be driving far.

Dr. Lewis: But we're scientists! We have no room for bias or opinions or judgment. We believe only in facts and figures and extrapolation of ideas from hard data. What business do people have believing our personal opinions on things?

Dr. Kelly: Because we're scientists...

Dr. Lewis: (groans) Jesus Christ....

Dr. Rumack: Dr. Lewis, I can understand what you're saying. You're saying what business does science have expressing an opinion; something that is not allowed in Science because emotions without data are nothing more than ignorant opinions?

Dr. Lewis: Yes, thank you! It just sounds like we're being pessimistic toward humanity. How can we be sure that we will be the means to our own destruction?

Dr. Rumack: Because the soil of a man's heart, Lewis, is stonier...

Dr. Lewis: That sounds familiar.

Dr. Rumack: It's from Pet Semetary.

Dr. Blair: Yeah, it is! Good quote, dude!

Dr. Rumack: Thank you. I wanted to save that, but I was worried that one of you guys would beat me to the punch so I had to say it.

Dr. Blair and **Dr. Kelly:** (complimenting Dr. Rumack on his wit, sounds of high-fives)

Dr. Rumack: ....you guys can feel free to use it, just remember that I said it first.

Dr. Kelly: Hey, you guys want to have a movie night?

Dr. Blair: Yeah, a movie night! II haven't seen Pet Sematary in a long time!

Dr. Kelly: We can have it at my house; I have sleeping bags.

Dr. Rumack: That does sound fun! Dr. Lewis, will you be joining us?

Dr. Lewis: I don't know, this is a lot to take in...

Dr. Rumack: It sounds like somebody doesn't want their Legion of Doom uniform...

Dr. Lewis: Well, no, I mean, I want the uniform...

Dr. Rumack: Great! We'll see you tonight at Dr. Kelly's. Bring popcorn and the movie, okay?

Dr. Lewis: Okay, I will. Wait, what about the clock? What are we going to set it at?

Dr. Rumack: Shit, I don't know. Fuck it. Put it at 11:56. I don't care. Oh, and Dr. Lewis?

Dr. Lewis: Yes?

Dr. Rumack: Blu-Ray, okay? None of that DVD nonsense.

My Last Day Teaching Kindergarten

Okay, kids! Kids, play-time is over, please put your toys away neatly in the play bin. Do it nicely, don't be jerks about it, and sit down on the carpet. Five seconds, guys! 4....3....2....1. Okay, good!

Now, can you remember what letter we learned yesterday? I'm pointing to it right here on the board. Gerald, don't stare at me with your mouth open, it's rude. Yes, Tracy, "W!" And what sound does the letter W make?

Wa....wa....wa....wa... and with that sound you can make out words like, What, Why, When... I know I got a little sidetracked yesterday with the letter W when I used Nietzsche's Will to Power as well as the Eternal Return of the Same. That was some heavy stuff to lay on you guys and I apologize. But just remember, the Eternal Return of the Same is merely a thought experiment to accompany the Will to Power. It does not necessarily mean that since time is eternal it is inevitable that you will be born again and will live the same life you are living now, the question is: Will you be okay with that if it were true? Carpe Diem, is basically what he is saying there.

Of course, you can also counter that argument by saying that time is a manmade construct and everything that ever has and will happen not only has already occurred, but has occurred all at once. Again, I leave you to ponder that on your own time.

Gerald, (snaps fingers) get your thumb out of your nose.

And today we are going to learn about the letter X! Isn't that fun, kids! The letter X. Now, the letter X isn't used too often; in fact, it is the third least used letter in the alphabet behind Q and Z.

Advertisers love the letter X because of its rarity and actually thinks the public will buy something because it has an X on it. X is like the bad boy of the alphabet. X will be late for his date with V, but it won't matter because he has a cool car and a leather jacket and V will still give X a hand-jibber at the very least even though V can still smell Y on his aXis.

That's a joke, kids.

Shoot, X won't even have to bother taking V out to dinner first. The hand-jibber will just manifest itself by the way X carries itself. But I, myself, am getting carried away.

Listen, the letter X can be used in such words as, "e<u>X</u>cellent," and "e<u>X</u>ceptional," two words that I am sure your parents use to describe you all the time to others, even though most of us know that it simply isn't true. Look at it this way: if everyone was exceptional, nobody would be. Think about that, okay? Think about it.

Not many words start with the letter X, however. There's "Xenophobia" which is a fear or hatred of foreigners. For instance, in the 1800's, there was a hatred of the Irish people coming over to this country and the Irish were sometimes called "White Negroes," which is pretty oxymoronic. Hey, there's another X word! But if there were such a thing as White Negroes, honestly, wouldn't they be those imperialist European douchebags in South Africa who practiced apartheid among other atrocious things? Wouldn't that, technically, be a "White Negro," that is, a white person from Africa?

People are terrible, is what I'm saying, kids, because just about every group has been hated by at least one other group of people. Hate derives from fear. Fear from ignorance.

Now, you might be thinking, a word like

Xenophobia, it doesn't sound like a typical "X" sound, and that's true! It sounds like a "Zee" sound, and you know what? You're right. And I'm not going to try to eXplain this away. You're just going to have to roll with it. This will not be the last time in your life where you will notice that English, as a language, is pretty fucked.

FluXed! I said fluxed. Got an X in it. Flux means to flow. Language flows. It's an organism, really. Now, I was debating on how best to demonstrate the letter X to you kids, so for the rest the of the class we will be watching the 1979 classic from Ridley Scott, *Alien*, starring Tom Skerrit. It is a classic example of a <u>Xenomorph</u>. If you haven't seen *Alien* or *Aliens* in your 6 years spent on this planet, then so far, you have failed in life, but that's okay. We're about to fi<u>X</u> that!

Jesus, How am I Going to Segue This Story of a Raped and Killed 7-Year-Old Girl Over to the Weekend Weather Report?

Ok, Bill, it's show time. Let's report this news.

Hello, and welcome back. I'm Bill Tannen. The search for missing 7-year-old Kayla Myers reached its tragic end today when her body was discovered at the bottom of...

Goddamn, this is some shitty news. What a shitty news day in general: unemployment on the rise, shooting spree at the local Wal-Mart, and now this dead kid shit.

...Kayla had been missing since last Tuesday after witnesses spotted her getting into an unmarked van...

Wait, why the hell are we reporting this story right after a commercial break? We should be going right to a commercial after I'm done reporting this. Unless...unless we're not going to a commercial. Why the hell wouldn't we go to a commercial right after this story? Where can we go from here? The weather? Fuck, it's the fucking weather, isn't it?

...Residents of the town are shocked and dismayed at the tragic news...

How the holy hell am I going to end this report and start back to the weather. Yep, there's my producer hand signaling that the weather report is next. What an asshole. He's been out to get me ever since I made that racial slur at the Christmas party. How was I supposed to know that his wife was Jewish? She didn't look Jewish.

Police are looking for anyone with any knowledge about the whereabouts of the culprit of this heinous...

HOW ARE WE NOT GOING TO A COMMERCIAL AFTER THIS? Oh, unless it's a commercial for St. Jude's Hospital. God, wouldn't that be so fucked? Alright, you can do this Bill. Dig deep. It's going to take all the experience and anchorman skill you got in your bag of tricks to make this work.

...where you can make donations to the family for funeral services. And now the weather!

Welcome to the Fleshlight Family!

Dear Sir,

My name is Henry Mills and I would like to personally thank you for your recent purchase of my life-long invention, the Fleshlight. Inside your package you will find a hand written certificate of authenticity and individual serial number for which to validate your purchase's legitimacy. And like all Fleshlights, this one has been *rigorously* hand tested before being allowed to ship to you, our highly valued customer!

As a Fleshlight customer, you are acknowledging the brilliance of my invention and are probably aware of the story of how a power outage in my home one night opened the door to a whole new world of self-satisfaction and further reluctance to talk to women. The idea itself evolved over the years, as most great inventions do. It started primitively as the CunnyCandle, then onto the OilDamp, followed by...well, if you do not know of the story, I have included it in the back of this welcome kit, on the page proceeding maintenance as well as the step-by-step methods for the recommended biannual cleaning of your Fleshlight.

Personally, I would not like to say that I am as dazzling or innovative as Edison or Jobs, but you and I both know that I am. This landmark invention wasn't as simple as finding the similarities between a female sex organ and an empty flashlight battery canister, no, no, no. There's a business end to this, and that is where my battle began. Do you know how many board rooms I was laughed out of when pitching my invention? I couldn't even tell you how many. It was a struggle, convincing people that I had reinvented the wheel. But thanks to people like you, we are proving to all of them that there is no point to using your hand when you have a velvety silicone tube in which to put your dick into. You sir, are a trendsetter!

And as a trendsetter, it is up to you to spread the word of this miraculous invention. Inside your Fleshlight, I have packed it to the labia with bumper stickers to put on your car or your desk at work as well as a Fleshlight t-shirt to wear whilst traipsing through the park or grocery shopping. Don't let others remain ignorant in their brainwashed, default ways of masturbating.

To think, people still use their hands for this stuff. Some guys even get girlfriends or wives. It's like, hello! It's the 21st century: stick your dick into a silicone tube!

Enjoy your Fleshlight. I hope you have as much fun using it as I did inventing it. Thank you and happy tubing!

Signed,

Henry Mills

That Clock is Slow, Just Like Your Son

Ah, Mr. and Mrs. Jenkins, please have a seat. How are you on this lovely day? I take it you are here to discuss the eligibility of your son, Michael, to attend this fine university?

I have perused your son's transcripts, along with his essay numerous times, and...you know what I love doing? I love spinning in my chair. Yep. I love spinning in my imported Italian Leather chair and looking around my fine, well-established office.

There's lots of things that make my office so admirable. I love looking at my numerous diplomas on the wall, along with my fine collection of academic books that I have either written myself, or have read and can recite verbatim. I love the appearance of how the early morning light casts itself upon my original Van Gogh painting, and how the evening light fades itself away on this bear-skin carpet that I killed in the Rocky Mountains back in '74. I have dedicated my life to this office, but there is just one thing here that doesn't fit: this clock here, situated on my desk before you.

This clock, I'm afraid, is terribly slow. Although it appears flawless, and carries a heavy weight of aesthetic pleasure, it is constantly giving me the wrong time, and therefore, giving me poor, misjudged information. It makes me chronically late for meetings, classes, and the like.

Believe me, Mr. and Mrs. Jenkins, I have tried to fix this poor teller of time on several occasions. I have changed its batteries, I have set it ahead of Eastern Standard Time. I have even taken it to a number of jewelers, hoping to fix its inner-workings in order to give me the correct time, and subsequently, make it "fit" among my already pristine office. But, alas, no one can seem to help me, and good heavens, I don't know what I shall do! All I know is that it doesn't belong here, that's for sure.

I am thinking of maybe sending it to my friend, Warren Potter. He's the head of the community college over in Montgomery County. Hey, you're from Montgomery County, aren't you? At any rate, I believe I am going to mail Warren this clock. I know his office well, have visited him several times, and I know that it would look best on his desk, not mine. It's a harsh reality that I am just going to have to succumb to, I'm afraid.

Well, thank you very much for your...haha...time, Mr. And Mrs. Jenkins. I bid you good day, and good luck.

To Whoever Was Using This Glory Hole

What's up, fellas! How are you guys doing? Enjoying the hole? The *glory* hole? I hope so. That was the intention as proclaimed by the glory hole mission statement here on the stall wall: "To be a glorious and gloried upon hole of mysterious pleasure." I know it sounds kind of vague, but if you look at the size and placement of the hole you'll realize that it's not like you're going to put your ear to it and hear the ocean. Unless putting your ear to things gets you off, then more power to you. But watch out! With this particular seashell, the ocean might give your ear a wet little kiss.

As most of you might realize, this is the fifth consecutive month of the Worm Hole's operation (That's the name, in case you didn't know, The Worm Hole.) And as much as I would like to have a big bash to celebrate, I realize that might contradict the principle of the Hole itself, which is sexy anonymity. We have seen and felt many great things in the past 5 months, my fellow Wormers, and I thank you kindly for your patronage of this particular glory hole. I do seriously believe that this hole will be standing long after any new rest areas are erected on this highway.

This hole is strong.

However, much like any glory hole worth its salt, there are some concerns I would like to address for the Hole's betterment. These are relatively simple matters and should make an already exhilarating experience that much more satisfying. I trust you to prick up your ears, gentleman, and listen to what I have to say.

The first issue is the sloppy floors. I know I sound like a broken record here with this issue, but it's true: the floors are a mess. And don't try to give me the excuse that it's from folks who are there to just use the bathroom. I'm so tired of hearing that. There is a *heavy* concentration of moisture around and under the hole itself, and last I checked, glory holes do not sweat. Every time I walk in here to change the velvet lining, I look like Bambi on the frozen pond and I nearly break my neck! So, please. Keep it dry, guys.

Secondly, I'm noticing some half-hearted attempts at the making of another hole on this stall. I don't know who is doing it, but it's completely unnecessary. Please don't waste your time. I really don't see the point of having two holes in the same wall. If you want to create your own glory hole somewhere else, more power to you! But please, don't try to ride the coattails of my hole. It's flattering, but you have little idea what you're doing.

Do yourself a favor and give this wall a rap with your knuckle. That's type 304 stainless steel, buddy! With a #4 satin finish for additional rigidity. You know how I know that? I'll tell you how: From the constant trips of going to Home Depot with manual hand drills that were all busted to shit. You know how many hand drills I went through? Three. Three times I had to go back to the store until finally I just asked the guy flat out, "You know that bathroom in the Arby's up by 202? What the hell are those stalls made of?"

So please, find your own wall to break through.

Finally, we come to a matter of professional etiquette. I know you guys are in a big hurry and don't really take the time to appreciate your surroundings or maybe your initial feeling of shame washes over you after you partake in the Hole and you rush out hastily, but please, *please* stop knocking over the candy dish. I don't know who exactly is doing it, but in my head, it's not a whole bunch of you guys actually doing it, and maybe I'm taking this too personally, but I feel as though it's just one person. One guy (or girl, fingers-crossed?) who spitefully takes a look at my effort and style and purposely knocks over the candy dish. It's a really disrespectful thing to do. My wife worked hard on that candy dish from her pottery lessons at the community college and you're sullying it with your disregard. Shame on you, sir (or madam!)

Is it the particular candy you do not like? Is that what's causing this? I've always had a fondness for Werther's and licorice, but that's just me. Hey, if you would like something else, just name it. I'm open to public opinion. After all, I did punch a hole through a stainless steel wall not just for *my* benefit, but for everyone's. So, what would you like? Runts? Laffy Taffy? Necco Wafers? Charleston Chew? Just let me know, guys.

And also, if you could, please try to remember to sign the guest book either on your way in or your way out. I know there's more people visiting than what the guest book says. Happy Holing!

...And You Can Tell Mr. Phelps I'm Way Too Cowardly to Say These Things to His Face!

You're bringing me *another* TPS form to fill out? Geez, what is this? And let me guess, this is another *brilliant* idea brought about by our illustrious leader, Mr. Phelps; the man who has the tenacity and the foresight to bring this company screeching to a devastating halt and then slowly burying it into the ground with paperwork.

I'm being facetious, you see.

Yeah, but no, you can tell him that. Yeah. Why don't you tell him that? Tell him that all of this paperwork he is making us do is unnecessary and that we are all doing as he says because his name is on our paychecks so nobody will stand up to his idiocy. Tell him!

Don't you think it's a tad absurd that after he took over this company we have been working more and getting less done? A lot of it has to do with the TPS reports, because mostly I think he made them just to feed his massive ego.

Somebody should tell him that! I certainly won't!

But you tell him he is being ridiculous with all this paperwork. You go ahead and tell him that for me. Tell him, "Bertram in Accounts has had enough of your pretentious bullshit," then come back and tell me what he says to *that!* I got him there. He won't have any comeback for that.

Well, *somebody* ought to tell him that, and I am much too cowardly to do it myself. But I can talk a big game, oh yes sir I can! From the safe confines of my office, with the door shut and my back to the wall so he can't sneak up on me, I can confidently tell you to tell him that this company is not what it used to be and that he is responsible for it.

The writing's on the wall!

Because honestly, I don't think you will do it. I don't think you will go right up to Phelps and tell him all of this shit that I am laying on you, and in reality, I am hoping that you won't. God help me if you actually tell Mr. Phelps how much I hate him and his stupid policies. But I know you won't, but you should know that I am angry about these policy changes and just know that if *I* were in charge, okay, If *I* were in charge, this company would be flying high and Phelps would be out on his pompous, naval-gazing ass.

I tell you this knowing full well that you have absolutely no pull with this company and cannot make any changes whatsoever. And if you do tell Phelps all of this stuff, he might come sniffing around to fire me, but I will wholeheartedly deny all of it, because I am a total fucking coward who sleeps in the fetal position. Hell, for the first few minutes after you leave my office, I am going to crawl underneath my desk and breathe into a paper bag, but don't tell him I said that, ok?

Oprah Interviews the Author of This Book

Mikey J, thank you so much for taking time out of your very busy schedule to meet on my show.
It's my pleasure, Oprah. Jimminy Glick cancelled, so...

Well, thank goodness for that! So tell me, what is happening with you?
To start, I just got off of another shift at work.

How intriguing! What is that like?
To put it modestly, I watch the rolls of film go around and around and around and around and around...like sands through the hourglass, so are the days of our lives.

That sounds so poignant.
I wish I could take credit for it, but it is actually from a soap opera.

Really? Which one?
General Hospital.

And at work, you're working with an all-star cast! Let's see...there's your group leader,

Kyle, and your supervisor, Anthony....
And don't forget about Jerry the Crack Addict.
Well, former crack addict. But he's showing
promising signs of relapse: you know, nodding off
in mid-sentence, falling asleep on the moving
forklift, constantly short of money, things of that
nature.

And he is your boss, he tells you what to do?
Yep. Uh-huh. And it's not like I can go to anyone
else about this. My group leader believes in
mermaids and my manager has a second job
where he moonlights as an alcoholic.

I'm sorry, mermaids?
Yeah. He watched a "documentary" on Animal
Planet about the existence of mermaids and he
didn't read the disclaimer that said that the
program was for entertainment purposes only,
and bam: we got mermaids.

**In case anyone has been living under a rock
for the past few weeks, the world was
aghast to hear that you had rats in your
luxury studio apartment. Would you like to
talk about that?** I knew you
were going to bring up the rats, Oprah. It's ok.
Everywhere I go, people ask me about the rats. At
least here I am able to reach quite a number of
people and I can clarify the story. The tabloids
reported that I had rats, whereas the New York

Times, Washington Post, Chicago Tribune...they got the story right. It wasn't a herd of rats in my suite; it was mice. There's a difference. You see, a rat will gnaw your face off with reckless abandon whilst you sleep, whereas a mouse will delicately place its turds throughout your apartment and give you a terrible feeling of malaise, nothing more.

How interesting! I did not know that!
That's why I'm here: to educate. At any rate, at first I only saw one mouse, and I named him Maxwell. After I broke his spine with a snap-trap, I found out that Maxwell wasn't the only one. I also ended up killing his brother Tony, his cousin/wife Debra, his sister/wife Genevieve, his Uncle Raymond, and his mother/wife Peggy. Six in total.

Michael, you lead such an interesting life! I'm so jealous!
(smirks dryly) I know. I'm sorry, but I really don't have much time here. I'm due back at my second job where I park golf carts, so...

My apologies. I understand how busy you are. I won't take up too much more of your time.
Good, because those carts won't park themselves, ya know?!

I'm sorry. Not much longer.
It's—it's—it's---it's---it's just that I'm the one in the cart barn, and it's my ass out there, ok?

I also understand that you finally told the woman you love how you feel. Would you like to talk about that?
What? How did you find out about that? That *just* happened.

(Reading text) "I love you. I want to marry you and start a family with you." Is that accurate? Is that what you said to her?

(Winces)

Boy, you really put it all out there, didn't you?

(Head between knees, groans)

Tell me, Michael, how did you think that would go? Because just by going by the first part of this interview and what you have to offer (rats, crack addicts, and mermaids), you will probably never see her again.

She said she'd think about it! That's got to count for something, right?

When did she say she'd think about it, Michael?

Right before she got in her car and…sped off.

And she blew past a stop sign as well, didn't she?

I don't want to talk about this, Oprah.

Okay, I understand. Let's talk about that book you self-published last year! Your last and most prosperous royalty check came in at $9.18…

This interview is over, Oprah.

Fair enough. Thank you very much for your time, Michael. Up next: A grown man who believes in mermaids! Find out how not reading one disclaimer can change your whole world-view.

Greetings From the Nickelback Fan Club!

Greetings and salutations to all of you out there in the world of Nickelback fandom! As you may be aware, it is the month of May and that can only mean that summer music tour season is nearly underway, which means that Nickelback, in all of its frothiness, deciduousness, and godliness will be coming to a town near you!

Yesssssssssss!!!

However, this issue of the Nickelback fan club newsletter will focus mainly on the slanderous things being said about the band. Hopefully, together, we can dispel these nasty rumors and just get back to some hard-core Canadian rocking. So let's take a look at what numerous blogs and news organizations have been saying about the greatest band since Ratt.

Rumor #1:

Chad Kroeger, lead singer of Nickelback, sings like he's got a mouthful of dicks.

First off, from a strictly semantic point of view,

it is really difficult if not impossible to stick more than one full dick in your mouth, ok? And then to assume that he, Chad Kroeger, can talk—let alone sing---let alone rock---while having his mouth full of dicks? Please. Through watching several hours of live concert footage and behind-the-scenes studio sessions, I can assure you that there was not a single solitary dick in Chad's mouth when he sang. **Rumor untrue!**

Rumor #2:

Chad Kroeger wouldn't know a good song if it shit on his face

Where to even start with this one, goodness! First off, let's dissect this statement. "Wouldn't know a good song." Well, that is just absurd. Of course Chad knows what a good song is. Have you seen all of the number one rock hits he pumps out year after year? Chad doesn't know a good song. Ha! Yeah, right, and Fred Durst doesn't know how to rap.

Secondly, how does a song go about defecating on someone? How does a song, which is nothing but noise, manifest itself into a living being that can not only seek out and find Chad, but to also render him helpless while this being releases its bodily functions all over him? Rumor untrue!

Rumor #3:

Chad Kroeger falls asleep to the sounds of slaughtering pigs for musical inspiration

Well, that's just…somewhat true. But it's not pigs. It's lambs. The slaughtering of little baby lambs.

Rumor #4:

Chad Kroeger sucks dick

Hmmm…I thought I had answered this accusation at the start of the Nickelback Fan Club Newsletter, but that only referred to what is in Chad's mouth when he sings. This particular accusation refers to a dick being placed in Chad's mouth for recreational purposes and not to improve his singing abilities. Look, it is impossible to know what a person is up to all 24 hours a day, even if we are talking about the biggest celebrity in the Canadian hemisphere: Chad Kroeger. He could easily go to a party in the Yukon with some hot babes, do some blow, then step into the bathroom and suck a quick dick. I don't know, ok? I just don't know. But I do know this: Chad Kroeger is not a homo. Homos are fags. Except for the ones who buy Nickelback albums. Those homos are alright. Chad ain't no homo, but if he were to suck dick, I'll tell you something: he would totally rock at it!

Next month we will return to our normal format and I will offer all of you Nickelback fans tips on how to live your Nickelback fandom to its fullest! Topics will include:

- The proper way to turn your bedroom speakers outward so the world can know how much you rock
- I will explain why buying 6 of every Nickelback album is a wise investment
- And I will teach you how to properly troll the Jr. High parking lot while listening to Nickelback music

Until then, folks, let's just keep on rocking! And let's keep buying those albums!!

Signed,

C. K.

Chad Kroeger, president, founder, head editor of the Nickelback Fan Club

Welcome to the Office, Champ

Why, hey there, guy! Welcome to the office! I'm Larry Neushwander; perhaps Mr. Phelps has told you about me. No? Well, first let's hear about you: what's your role here? No, not, "shipping and receiving." I'll ask it again: what is your *role* here, friend?

Don't take too much time to think about it. Here, take a look at my tie. It's goofy, right? It's like a gag tie of some sort, with lights on it, funny sequins, maybe even a little interactive. Why don't you tug on the tongue there. Whoop! Say, what happened?? Hahaha, right???

And you're probably thinking, "Why wear such an odd, goofy tie? What's the special occasion?" Well, I'll lean in close and whisper it to you.

It's Tuesday.

You see, buddy, I'm the Office Cut-Up, and with that title I don't need some fanciful excuse to don a tie such as this. This is average for me. Why, to wear a regular tie would be out of character. People wouldn't recognize me! I'd walk past them and they'd be like, "Hey, have you seen Larry today?" And I'd be all, "Larry? That jerk? He owes me money!" Nyuk Nyuk!

Now, listen here, kid: I don't know what back-alley office you crawled out of or what your role was there, but here, I am Larry the Jokester. I ease away office tension through a random assortment of movie quotes, sarcastic non-sequiturs, and pratfalls.

Pratfalls are my specialty.

Of course, that is not to say that I am not thinking of the perfect Forrest Gump quote to end this conversation, but that will be later. Don't try to predict it, but you should know that it is coming.

You're going to see me camped out at the water cooler quite frequently, as that is my hunting grounds. Feel free to come on over and discuss with me last night's episode of the most popular sitcom! Chances are I will have the punch-lines memorized and on the ready to recite back to you at a moment's notice. Hey, it's what I do. Just don't you try to do it too, alright?

Now, I'm not trying to discourage you from being yourself, ok? I'm not wholly against a little help when I make my jokes. Sometimes my comedy gets a little edgy and I have to kick-start the laughter myself to let the others know that it's okay. It happens frequently when I quote Buckwheat from *The Little Rascals.*

Buddy, I think we are going to get along great if you simply respect the boundaries around here. I look forward to making you laugh and am looking forward to the challenge of getting a guffaw out of ya. And that's all I have to say about...that. Nailed it!

Oh, and stay away from Robin Williams quotes. They're mine. All of them, you got that?

Alright, Which One of you Assholes Stole My Jock Jams Volume II CD?

Ok. Ha ha. Very funny, guys. Very funny. I suppose it is kind of humorous, I guess. Yes, right now I am without my Jock Jams volume II CD. Hardy har har. I see you stifling your laughter, Charles. Did you take it? Huh? Was it you? I'll bet it was. Charles, you always pull shit like this. Well, if it wasn't you, who was it? Huh? Which one of you assholes was it?

It couldn't have simply been misplaced. I refuse to accept that notion, Randy. Come on, guys. It's not that hard of a CD to miss. It's got bedazzled jewels on the casing, some glitter, and oh yeah, it's the greatest cd of all time!

This is volume II, assholes. Volume II of the Jock Jams canon was by far the strongest. The first volume was just a feeler; a reconnaissance mission of what we jocks jam to. After accumulating feedback and knowing our likes and dislikes, ESPN went back to the drawing board and formed the perfect album. By Volume

III the fame went to their heads and there was no going back. And what about Volume IV, you ask? Please.

You're jealous that I have it and you don't. That's the only reason I can fathom. We were all having a nice time tonight, weren't we? We got out the Turning Leaf white wine, having a lovely dinner, catching up with friends, their wives and children...but the dinner party really got started when I snuck that CD into the stereo. What were we listening to before that? Dan Fogelberg? More like Dan FAG-elberg! Haha! Am I right? C'mon, Tommy. Up high.

I saw the looks on your faces when you heard the voices of Sports Center announcers Dan Patrick and Chris "The Swami" Berman welcome us "To the Big Show" on track number one. You all had this look on your faces that was like, "Damn! Why didn't I think to bring my CDs to the party?" Maybe you will next time we get together. Maybe. If you're smart. But we all brought a little something to the dinner party, didn't we? Kyle, you and your wife brought that Mediterranean dish with the noodles and shit. Steve, you brought that new version of Trivial Pursuit for us to play after dessert. Lola, you made that lovely table centerpiece that held the salt and pepper. And as for me, well, I brought the fuckin' intensity!

You do know that this CD is part of my daily routine, right? I listen to it in the car on my way to gym. I put it in my disc-man while I am at the gym, and I turn it way the fuck up when I am in the tanning bed and just totally jock-jam out. Where else can you find an album that contains both Coolio and The Village People? I ask you this even though I know there is only one answer. If you think it is funny to take that kind of joy from me, then fine. Go right ahead. I can lead an empty life. No problem. Some friends you are.

. . .

. . .

I cannot believe I am this close to completely losing my shit because of some dumbass fuck game of hide and seek! I am fucking pissed!! Give it back! Right fucking now! I swear to fucking Christ I will castrate your fucking asses if I don't get that CD back! I will single-handedly rip your dicks off and shove them down each other's throats, and I will make you say that you love it!!

ROOOOOOOOOAAAARRRRRRR!!!!!

You know what?! Don't give it back! Because if you give it back to me right now, I will turn that shit up to 11 and it will be the anthem to your own sick destruction!! Fuck this! And fuck all of you!!

Before We Begin

Hello, everyone. I would like to thank you all for coming over to our house this Thanksgiving. Martha, my dear, the turkey looks wonderful! I don't think I have ever seen a bird as succulent in all my life. I can't wait to dig in. But, before we begin this festive meal, I would first like to apologize to you all for my behavior the last time we saw each other.

Has it been six months already since the "Incident"? I suppose it has, and after that embarrassing display of anger on my part, the shame will not really go away no matter how long ago it was. I went to therapy for my anger problems, to identify the kindling for my fiery rage and after weeks and weeks of intense… well, never mind, I won't burden you with my problems, but I would like to apologize.

Carl, I am sorry that I called you derogatory names six months ago. I was in a blinding fit of frustration and was later told that I called you such heinous names as "Beaver-Beater," and "Canuckle-Head." I always knew you were

Canadian, Carl, even before you married my sister, but I honestly didn't think it was going to be a factor when we were on the set of Family Feud. I was wrong, and I'm sorry. It took me by surprise that someone would say that in order to stay warm, one might put on their favorite pelt. I would think sweater or blanket, but no, apparently when there is a chill in the air, we reach for our most recently killed squirrel or raccoon.

Great Aunt Phyllis, my god am I ever sorry! We had no idea that dementia was already setting in on your twilight years, and the set of Family Feud in front of the McDonald family as well as Steve Harvey was not the place to find out. And it certainly wasn't the place for me to diagnose your condition as well as say that you were faking it. I should have known better that your behavior was not a personal attack on me as well as an attempt to embarrass me in front of thousands of people. Looking back on it, after knowing what we know about your condition, Aunt Phyllis, your answers were quite comical.

If Uncle Richard were here, I would apologize to him, but he has not responded to any of my messages. Such is the case when you threaten the life of somebody when the points are worth triple.

It's just…Family Feud is a really difficult show to get on, you know? The waiting list is, like, the length of my arm. Do you have any idea the hoops I had to jump through, the palms I had to grease in order to get us a spot? The producers decided not to air our episode (thank goodness!), but they did send me a copy. So, before we begin with this meal, I think it would behoove all of us to sit down and watch it and go over where each and every one of you went wrong. Martha, no, it's ok. I apologized to you earlier after not speaking to you for those six months. We're all good here. I just want everyone to see the embarrassment they caused me and themselves.

…Well, who's holding the carving knife, you or me? That's right: me. And I say we watch the tape. Carl, don't try to start talking now, you're only burying yourself deeper, you Eh-Hole. C'mon, let's go to the living room. I'll hold onto the knife, Martha, thank you.

Advice Column: Ask a Premature Ejaculator

DEAR PREMATURE EJACULATOR:
With Thanksgiving nearly a month away, my husband
and I are at odds as to which of our parents' houses we
will be visiting. This is our first Thanksgiving together as
a married couple and I want to get things off on the right
foot. How do we reach a compromise?
---Torn in Tallahassee.

Dear Torn:

When approaching this particular problem it is
best not to focus *too* much on the task at hand. Of
course, you want to be engaging with the
problem, but not completely absorbed. For
instance, if I were you, I would close my eyes and
think about baseball. Try to start at the first
inning of an imaginary game and go pitch by
pitch and see how long you can last before the
problem is solved.

DEAR PREMIE:
Last week my mother passed away. Since my father died
nearly ten years earlier, their estate has been left to me
and my two brothers, and all three of us have different
ideas on what to do with the property. Can you help?
---Stagnant in Seattle

Dear Stagnant:

Try wearing two condoms.

HEY, PRE-JACK:
My best friend just got engaged to a wonderful girl and
he asked me to be his best man. It is a great honor.
However, he is planning a destination wedding to a
faraway place and I don't have the financial means to
accompany him. How do I tell him this?
----Broke in Buffalo

Dear Buffalo:

Okhereiswhatyoudobutyouhavetolistentomever
ycarefully.
Thefirstthingyouneedtodois....OHHHHHHHH,
DEAR!!!

...

...

I am very sorry about that. That, uh, that's never
happened to me before. Honest. It's just...you had
a really great problem and I got a little excited.
You should...you should take it as a compliment,
really. Thank you. I'm sorry. Thank you. Now, if
you don't mind---I think I might have mentioned
it earlier---I have to get up early tomorrow, so I
think I am just going to head out...

I Interview Jake Steinfeld, A.K.A Body By Jake

Jake! I would like to thank you very much for taking the time to answer some of my questions.

Happy to be here, Michael. Nice place you have here.

Yeah, thanks, it's alright.

I especially like your random assortment of disposable cutlery.

Yeah, they spruce up the place quite nicely, I find. Jake! It is so good to see you! I can't believe you're here! I have so many questions.

Well, I'm here to answer them, so go right ahead.

Ok. Ok. Ok. Let's see...how are you?

Good! Good! I feel great!

How are your products moving along? I see that there are still products with your name on them, but your physical presence seems to have disappeared off of the infomercial scene.

. . .

...That... that's not a question, Michael. But I will discuss that. I am in my mid-fifties now, still in great shape of course, but I find that my brand name goes a lot farther than just my working out on the equipment. I still do the voice-over work. That is something I have always enjoyed. But for instance, for one of my latest products, the Tower 200, we got celebrity spokesman, 5-time MMA Champion Randy "The Natural" Couture to endorse our product.

Wow! MMA Champion!

5-time Champ, yeah.

That's very exciting! Quick question: What is MMA?

Mixed Martial Arts. What did you think it stood for?

Let's not... I'm glad you named the Tower 200 specifically. I have so many questions regarding this product.

Go for it!

Ok, first and foremost: I have a door. Does this also imply that I have a gym?

Yes! That's the beauty of the Tower 200 by Body by Jake! Anyone with a door and 11 minutes on their hands has their own gym. Isn't that fantastic?

Yes, it truly is! What about a swinging kitchen door like the one from the set of ALF? Will that work?

Ah, no. I don't think it will. In fact, you will probably repeatedly smack the door against your head with up to 200 pounds of explosive resistance.

And the beaded curtains I have for my bathroom door; I assume this is no good.

That is correct. The beads don't actually act as a physical door, more of a cover for the doorway of your bathroom.

I'm learning so much, Jake.

Hey, that's why I'm here. Here's the kind of doors the Tower 200 works on: House, office, and dorm. That's why the slogan goes, "Gotta door? You gotta gym!"

Oh, shit! I see it now. "Gotta" as in "Got A" not, "Got to."

Right. Exactly.

I was way off! Oh, man, honest, like, 85% of my confusion—gone. Ok, so is it safe to say something like, "I gotta workout. Fortunately, I gotta door, so I in turn gotta gym."

Michael, I think you've got it. Plus, it's padded, so there's no messing up your door.

But my door isn't padded. Will this mess up my gym?

No, it will not. The padding will protect both your gym and your door. I think you would really benefit from one of these fine products. I got one out in my car, why don't we set you up with one? It's risk-free for just $14.95.

Eh, I don't know, Body by Jake, I did a couple pushups a few months ago and I'm still coming down from that burn.

Michael, look at you. You weigh what, 160 pounds?

163.

And you've got arms like a dead eel. Let me just go get a Tower 200 real fast and see how you like it.

Body by Jake, I gotta be a straight-shooter here: I've been hitting the box wine pretty hard today, and I really think if I were to exercise I would release vomit and bowel with 200 foot-pounds of explosive non-resistance.

What a sight you are.

Look, Franzia gave me the courage to conduct this interview. I was really nervous.

You're still shaking like a weak Chihuahua. I wouldn't say that's nerves, more like malnutrition.

You should have seen me before I ate that handful of peanut brittle.

Well, look, it's been real, but I should really get going. I hope I answered all your questions.

You did, Mr. Steinfeld. You sincerely did not disappoint. Let me walk you to the front gym—I mean, door! Gah! I keep doing that.

So, I'm Thinking About Getting a Leg Tattoo

I've been entertaining the idea of getting a leg tattoo for quite some time now. I don't know what it is about a leg tattoo; perhaps it's the vivid coloring, the shaved leg hair around the ink, or the fact that it is hardly seen in the winter time. But once Spring comes... well, no, it's still kind of chilly in Spring, but Summer...oh, man, in Summer time I'm going to bust out the cargo shorts and my leg tattoo will just make my calf pop with intimidation and visceral male virility!

The leg tattoo is a seasonal artwork, much like any deciduous conifer in the autumn season. Of course, if I go through with the leg tattoo, phrases and terms such as "deciduous conifer" will have to be replaced with something like, "tree."

It may seem that I am simply getting some ink done on my leg, but that is not the case, not with a leg tattoo, no, no, no. A leg tattoo invokes a certain attitude, a certain *je ne sais quoi*. Anyone can get an arm tattoo or a tramp stamp on the lower back, but the leg tattoo crowd has only a few select people to which I would love to be a part of and that means that certain sacrifices will have to be made.

The first thing I am going to have to do is break up with my current girlfriend. The reasons are obvious I'm sure, but I will spell it out for you. Most importantly, I will be at a much higher level of attraction post leg tattoo, so whoever I was with beforehand will look like dirty street trash compared to me and my leg. I can't be with someone who is so blatantly unattractive standing next to my ink. It's not fair to me, it's not fair to her, and it's not fair to my now sexy calf. The other reason I will have to break up with my current girlfriend is because her name is not Tonya. Or Chanice. Or Cookie. Or Skye. Or Desiree. Or Jasmyn. Or Mysty. Or Dani. Or Candi.

You might be asking yourself, "Mike, aren't these all stripper names?" And I will tell you, yes, yes they most certainly are! I never fancied myself a guy who would spend a lot of time in a strip club, but after this leg tattoo, who knows? Maybe I will have the confidence to date a girl who grinds herself up on strangers all night. Perhaps I will just sit in the corner of the club with my cup of tobacco spit and casually threaten the customers who hit on her. And remembering my girlfriend's name won't really matter since I will only refer to her exclusively as, "Babe."

The biggest change I will experience after I get the tattoo will probably be that I am going to have to move to Florida; probably around the Tallahassee area in the pan-handle, someplace where I can cruise around on my 4-wheeler and light fireworks. If you want to throw a make-shift ramp into the mix, all the better. What I and my leg tattoo would really like to do is strap a shitload of bottle rockets around the frame of my four wheeler so that they ignite right before I hit the ramp that me and my friends built out of soggy, rotted tree limbs. I'll be fairly confident that my four wheeler will be mistaken for Doc Brown's time-traveling Delorean, but if something goes wrong and I hurt myself, I trust that my fellow leg tattoo enthusiasts will upload the video of the incident to YouTube before calling an ambulance, no matter how many times I say, "Bro, seriously! I'm serious bro, I'm hurt!"

Also, "bro" will become my pronoun of choice.

Then there's the crystal meth addiction. Amp. Blue belly. Crank. Crystal. Speed. White Cross. Go-Go Juice. Whatever you want to call the stuff, it walks hand in hand with the tattoo. I don't want to see it as a burden, even though I have never tried Go-Go Juice before, but these are the sacrifices you make when you get a picture of the

Windows 98 logo on your leg.

I also have no idea how to buy crystal meth. My only hope is that my leg tattoo will send a signal (a la Batman) to nearby dealers and they will come to me. Can you imagine how hot my tattoo will look in some decrepit motel room on the side of the highway where I use the bedbug-ridden comforter as a large curtain?

Chanice-- babe, go to the vending machine down the hall and get us some breakfast.

If this new lifestyle choice does put me on the wrong side of the law, I really hope that when I do get busted by the police I'm wearing shorts; that's all I ask.

Steve Guttenberg Contemplates Reprising His Role For Short Circuit 2

Hmmmm... *Short Circuit 2.* I don't know. I just don't know. *Short Circuit* was such a hit; are we sure we want to go back to that well again? There's so much to factor in here.

First of all, who is willing to come back for a sequel? I wonder if Ally (Sheedy) will sign back on. Fisher Stevens, I don't think he has anything on the horizon. As for Johnny #5, well, I can almost guarantee that he is going to be in it. In fact, this was probably all his idea anyway. Goddamn it, Johnny. I don't like being in this position.

Now, wait a second, wait a second. Since when do I, Steve Guttenberg, need to know who else is assigned to a film before I, Steve Guttenberg, consider it? Guttenberg *is* the film. Guttenberg takes the mundane and makes it his own. Just take a look at *Police Academy.* And now ask me what film I just put in the can 2 weeks ago. That's right-- *Police Academy 4: Citizens on Patrol.*

It's like, I know---I *know* that my work on *Police Academy 4: Citizens on Patrol* will seal me as a Hollywood icon for years to come. I know this. The question is, which film will make my career...*legendary?* Will it be *Short Circuit 2?*

Come on, Gutes! Think!

Then Guttenberg also has to worry about the plot itself. Where exactly can the Newton Crosby character go from here? Johnny #5, he's malleable, he can bend to any scene and make it his own, that's why I still believe that role should have been mine, but no matter. No matter! Do I want to make this sequel?

...

...

No, I don't. I simply don't. I'm going to have to go with my gute on this and my gute says no. I should wait around for a sequel to *Cocoon* or maybe a *Three Men and a Little Baby* sequel. That's the meal ticket. That's the stuff legends are made of.

I know there is no sense in worrying about it, but I can't help but be concerned that this new *Short Circuit* film might undercut all the hard work I did in the first one. To think of all that I put into that character. All of his brevity, his humanity, his philosophical whimsy and merriment, his porous sexuality… to think it could all be marred by another film!

Now granted, without the Guttenberg Seal of Approval, this movie is going to tank and I think the fans will know that. If they can just keep my character out of the new one completely, Guttenberg will be pleased. Fisher playing the role of Ben Jabituya, that was *hilarious* in the first one, but does he have the confidence, the strength, the talent, the-the-the-the-the *Guttens* to keep a whole film together for 89 minutes? You know what? It's their problem now. Guttenberg has passed, and now they must go upstream. Without a paddle. Or a boat. Or an A-list actor.

Pullin' the Pud: That Chick From the Progressive Insurance Commercials, Flo

It's difficult to go an entire day without coming across a Progressive Insurance advertisement and subsequently, their spokesperson; a chipper young lass by the name of Flo. Television spots, full page magazine ads, website banners, radio...she's everywhere! And, as a male, I am biologically obligated to mentally have sex with her. How would it go? What would it be like?

Flo is a pretty bland girl. She has no distinctly feminine body structure since she dresses all in white with a smock and she is so damn happy and upbeat, you'd figure the sex would be really encouraging. Even if you prematurely ejaculated she'd probably give you a reassuring pat on the back. But a pre-jac will be most unlikely considering her pansexual features. In fact, all we know about Flo is that she *loves* the company she works for and everything else would come a distant second in her life. The question must be asked, "How does one get into those starchy white pants of hers? How could I turn her on in my own imagination?"

So, I am in my corner office behind my grand oak desk, sitting in my buttoned leather chair. The office is fully furnished in fine mahogany, stained dark and it smells of old money. On the desk stands a name placard. It reads: *Michael Jenkins, President & CEO, Progressive Insurance.* I suddenly realize that anyone who is anyone probably already knows that and doesn't need a name card to identify myself if they are called into my office. I quickly throw the nameplate in the trash. The fireplace has a gentle flame going, but it is raising its intensity, like my lust: smoldering, ready to hiss and pop.

I press the intercom button and tell my receptionist, Janet, to let Flo into my office. (Janet is a wonderful receptionist, but a pretty weak lay, if I'm going to be honest with you.) Flo flows into my office, eyes wide with excitement. She is all smiles as per usual. I tell her to close the door and have a seat. I commend her on her diligence to bring my company up out of the cellar. She accepts the compliments with such modesty, claiming that she just loves saving people money on their insurance. She's so coy. She's so...Flo.

To demonstrate her passion on saving people money, she pulls out her price-zapping gun and shoots down any imaginary hidden fees and last minute taxes that the other companies are known for. She starts zapping near my collection of hand-made Pez dispensers and as she works her way over to my 1st edition Vonnegut novels, I put my hands up defensively. "Whoa, Flo! Whoa! Take 'er easy. Nice shootin',' but you needn't that pistol in here." I motion her to give me the price gun, and when she does hand it over, she also leaves herself open and vulnerable to my seductive ways.

I move out of my chair gracefully and tell her of some exciting new pricing bundles and insurance plans I would like her to represent. Her smile rolls over wide, her hands fisted and shaking with eagerness. Eagerness to sell.

Eagerness to please.

I place myself on the corner of my desk with my left leg dangling in front of Flo, letting her be aware that it is within touching distance.

I mention price bundles, deductibles, auto, home, life, renter's...her eyes loom large and her mouth salivates like a Pavlovian Dog. I tug at my pant leg and she mimics the action and reaches out to rub my leg. It's not me, it's the insurance that's doing this to her. And for some reason, I am quite ok with that.

The only challenge I can bring myself is to keep the conversation alive and electric. I am going to need to bring my full arsenal of insurance jargon to put this thing to the next level. She soon succumbs to my verbal swooning of interest rates and premium pricing plans and she takes the bait. The bait that is my penis.

As I clear off my desk with one fell swoop of my arm, I have to think about more insurance stuff to whisper into Flo's ear. It's going to be a monumental task to be sure: First, to talk insurance for the duration of the sexual encounter and secondly, sustaining an erection while talking about said insurance. I do know what I am going to save for the climax though. I am going to shout, "Full Medical! Full Medical!" Something like that.

Anyway, we proceed to have the most boring, palest sex imaginable, like indulging in a meal of white rice and skim milk.

Does This Feel Contagious To You?

Hey, honey. Can you come here for a sec? Here, in the bathroom. I've got this thing here...some sort of growth or pustule or something...

Wait. Close your eyes. Just follow my voice. Why not? Trust me. I swear it will be worth it. And no, it will not be like the "Dutch Oven" instance from last May. I cannot apologize enough for how terribly awry that went. This won't be like that, I promise. This will be different.

Come on, babe. Where's your sense of adventure? You know, you read all these chick magazines about how to spice up your love life and keep your marriage vibrant and here we are. Spontaneity is a-knocking at the door and it is up to you to answer it.

And if it is intimacy you're looking for, well, look no further! This is a perfect opportunity sharpen our intimacy edge.

Honey, I am literally oozing with intimacy.

I'm not going to tell you where it is; where's the

fun in that? We could make a game of it. A sexy, fun, adventurous marital game. We'll call it, "Does This Feel Contagious?" I'll light a few candles, we'll turn on some smooth jazz and you can tell me what the hell is growing on me and whether or not I can afflict others with it.

Now, hey, to be fair, I have offered to do your mammograms, but you were all, "I need a doctor to check," and I could tell that you weren't about to check me for shaft cancer, which is where the conversation was going to go inevitably, I'm not going to lie.

I honestly wonder where the hell this thing came from. The more it pulsates, the more concerned I seem to get. ...No, not my shaft, I'm getting kind of serious now. I'm talking about this growth. Try to keep up.

Remember in the movie *Creepshow* when Stephen King came across that meteor and he turned into some kind of giant weed or some shit?

...Well, maybe I *did* come across a meteor, you don't know. There was something in the back of the fridge that I couldn't identify, but I didn't eat *all* of it, just enough to let me know that I should throw it out. I'm just saying that the meteor shit in *Creepshow* was highly contagious and I just want to know what I am dealing with here.

Honey, if I go to the doctor, what am I supposed to write down on the form? "Growth with its own heartbeat, fear of becoming Jordy Verrel"?

Okay, I know I am going to sound like a dick here, but you can either feel this now with your hand and give me your opinion, or you can wake up in the middle of the night to feel it rubbing against your shoulders. The choice is yours. Will it help if I turn off the lights?

Your Cousins Are Hot, Dude

Hey, buddy. I see on Facebook that you went on a little family get-together up to the lake last week. Yeah, I saw the pictures. It looked like a good time. Did I see that you guys went on an old tire swing right over the water? That looked badass! Who did you hang out with up there? Your parents, your aunt and uncle... am I forgetting someone? Oh, that's right! Your cousins were up there too, right? Yeah, I think I saw a couple of photos of them in their bathing suits. There were three of them there, right? I might have glanced at the pictures for a few minutes, sure.

They're over 16, right? Yeah, I thought they were, I was just checking. I saw the photos of you guys riding go carts and was just wondering if they were of legal age; Legal age to drive go carts, that is. What are their names? Victoria, Tonya, and Stephanie? Okay, which one is the brunette? I see that there are two are blondes and one is a brunette. Okay, Stephanie is the brunette, that's good to know. Do any of them have boyfriends? No, wait, don't tell me.

But the lake looked like fun! I'm sorry your grandfather couldn't make it; angina's a bitch, bro. How come Tonya wasn't wearing a two-piece bathing suit at the lake? She certainly has the body type to pull off a bikini. She's fit, yo! There isn't any kind of scarring going on in the midsection, is there? Did she have appendicitis? Any kind of vicious stray dog or chimpanzee attack when she was younger? Did she get a really bad tattoo down there? If she has an appendectomy scar, tell her not to be self-conscious about it, okay? Appendicitis can be hot if it's done right.

You don't mind me talking about this stuff, do you? I'm sure you get it all the time when you're around those girls. Let's face it: your cousins are hot, dude.

Sure, we can talk about the lake and your family and your Mom and Aunt getting into a huge fight over the macaroni salad and blah, blah, blah... but I feel it's important to tell you just how hot your cousins are. No, I don't think it's a useless thing to say to you. Rubber baby bubble bumpers! That...haha... *that* is a useless thing to say. Where can the conversation go after I say something ridiculous like that? But if I say, "Your cousins are hot," there's a whole world of unexplored conversation we get to traverse!

Pack your bags, fella!

Firstly, we could rank the bangability of your cousins. One through three. You're going to want to know this, okay? See, what you have going on here is you've got two blondes and a brunette, so I think the wisest thing to do is put the brunette safely in second and bookend her with the blondes. If there was a red-headed cousin tossed into the mix, that would really throw me for a loop and this conversation could go on all night (I'm talking degree of paleness, as well as freckle concentration and placement) but your gene pool isn't that deep, so let's just move on.

Yeah, I'm sorry, *too.*

Well, how would *you* rank the hotness of your cousins? It's a simple question and you won't even answer me that. I'm leaning toward putting Tonya in third place only because of her monkey-paw scratches across her stomach. That only seems fair. Unless Victoria is a bitch, she is going to go in first place for me. Tell me she's a stone-cold bitch and I'll reconsider right here and now. But as of this moment, Victoria is ranked number one for me, okay? Shoot, who am I kidding? Bitchiness can be hot if it's done right. But if Stephanie comes along and asks you how I ranked them all, tell her I put her at number one, okay? She seems like a good kid and I don't want to hurt her feelings.

As for Tonya, tell her that there are procedures to get that tattoo of John McCain off of her rib. Unless the John McCain tattoo is done tastefully, Tonya is put in last place for me. Now, don't get me wrong-John McCain tattoos on the rib can be hot if it's done right, but it is very rare. Okay, so you have my final standings, right? Recite them back to me so I know for sure that you know.

A Lovely Little Dinner Party

Hey, folks! Come in! Come in! It's so good to see all of you! Step right this way. I have a lovely meal planned for all of us. Let's go through the hallway here and into the dining area where I have a full bar set up for us. Do you like the lights? I hope they don't blind you: 100 watt bulbs. Sorry, but I like to keep every crevice of the place well lit. I don't mind the high electric bill. Sorry, Samantha, I can't turn them off. Trust me, you don't want them turned off. ...Well, just don't look directly at the bulbs. Simple, right? Why don't you go get yourself a drink? Bill, how's that new insurance gig working out for ya? Are you highly...ac-claimed! Haha! Nyuk nyuk! I'll be right back with the salads.

...

...

Foot stomp! *Crash!** Spritz spritz!* (Loud shuddering)

...

...

Salad's here! Everyone sit, sit! Nancy, why

don't you regale us with that time you saw
Sylvester Stallone walking across the street. He
was really short, right? Like, tiny? Weird! I'm so
glad everyone could make it. And to think, I was
toying with the idea of cancelling. Oh, no
particular reason, really.

Hey, did you guys know that a cockroach can
live for an entire week without its head? True
story. Because of their open circulatory system,
they don't breathe strictly through their mouth
but through little openings all over its body. It will
actually die of thirst first without its head. Weird,
right? Anyone care for some more dressing?

Nick, didn't you have an insect infestation at
that place you moved into right after college? No?
I could have sworn you did. That must have been
someone else. Samantha, I'm just making
conversation; you don't need to read so much into
everything. I'm simply stating some factoids.
Like, did you know that you can kill a cockroach
with a simple spritz of soap and water? It's true!
The soapy water seals up the breathing pores of
the roach and they suffocate within, like, a
minute.

Nathan, I would *not* turn off that light if I were
you. Then switch seats if it's too hot near the
exposed bulb. You ever see that movie *Pitch
Black*, with Vin Diesel? Where there's a bunch of

creatures that only come out and feast at night? And there's that one scene where that chick lights up the flare and all these things scatter back real fast? That was a good movie. An accurate portrayal, in my opinion.

What's that, Nick? You said your salad tastes a little…"soapy"? I don't know what you're talking about.

Another thing regarding insects: did you know that people eat insects as a delicacy in over 130 countries worldwide? Wait, hold on. Let me get the entrees.

…

…

(Frantic spritzing) (Sounds of a personal struggle)

…

…

Okay, still a few more minutes on that lamb. But where was I? Nick, what do you mean you're leaving? You just got here! I'm sorry for the subject matter; it's just that I think if we as a country could get over our prejudices regarding our little exoskeletal friends…it's less methane than farming livestock and just as nutritious, that's all.

Samantha, don't leave. I'm only saying that if you ever found yourself biting into a cockroach, it wouldn't be the worst thing in the world. Bill, you too! Oh, come on! You haven't even finished your salads!

Nick, your salad leaf moved? Now you're just being dramatic. You've seen too many of those quirky comedy routines. Let me guess what happens next: my boss is about to give me the big raise I've been asking for, but first he takes a bite of the mobile salad, right? Right?? Well, I don't see Mr. Shirley here, do you? And to be honest, I don't think he'd mind a little accidental crunch in his salad.

I'm sure if you thought my kitchen was infested with kittens, you wouldn't be running out the door, would you? Would it help if I gave you all your own personal spray bottles with soapy water mix? Guys, please, don't leave! Mr. Shirley will be here any minute!

We Need to Talk About Kevin

Hey, gang. Could you gather around for a minute? Sorry, this will just take a minute. I don't like to bother you guys in the middle of a workday like this, but it's kind of important. Is that everyone? Okay, Terry? Terry, I love your dedication, but the T.P.S. reports can wait a few minutes, okay, pal? Thanks.

I've always said that I didn't want to just run a business, but I also wanted all of us who work here to be treated like family. And we are a family; we say 'hello' to each other by name when we pass each other in the halls, we have dinner over each other's houses, heck, we even have a softball team. Sure, we're in last place, but it's not about winning, it's about community and family. We support each other as best we can and we work toward a common goal. That's why I feel I can be straight with you and that's why we're having this meeting. It's about Kevin from Accounting.

I think some of you may have noticed that Kevin from Accounting hasn't been doing too well lately. He's been kind of sluggish, he's been forgetting key numbers, he can't burn the midnight oil with the rest of us like he used to… overall, he just isn't the same accountant that we knew and loved when he first came here. He was extremely bitter and agitated all the time. He just wasn't a joy to be around anymore. Most importantly, he brought down team moral. *Family* moral. That wasn't the Kevin we knew and loved! The Kevin we knew was boisterous, full of laughter and love, and most importantly, showed up on time and handed his timesheets in a timely manner. So, what the heck are we going to do about Kevin?

If you haven't noticed, Kevin hasn't been in the office since Monday. What we did, V.P. Daniel and I, we thought this over for a long, long time and what we decided to do was we give Kevin away to a nice Accounting Farm upstate somewhere.

It's for the best that Kevin is up there now because he wasn't happy here anymore. He had a hard time keeping up, his energy was quite low, his hair was thinning something awful, and his blood-pressure was through the roof; that doesn't make for a happy accountant, okay? We don't have a happy accountant and we don't get our timesheets handed in on time and then we don't get our paychecks and then we have an unhappy staff. It's better this way. Trust me, if it got to the point where you guys didn't get paid, *you* all would have taken Kevin out back behind the Goodwill clothing donation bin and shot him.

...

Not that Daniel and I took Kevin out to the Goodwill donation clothing bin in the parking lot and shot him. Like I said, we gave Kevin to a nice accounting farm.

"Where?" is a good question, Tom. I like your curiosity, I like your verve. Where is Kevin, exactly? Well, mentally, he was never here anyway, am I right? Hahahaha! Ok, I'm sorry, that was inappropriate. I think you mean to which accounting farm did we send him? Unfortunately, I do not have the exact address of this accounting farm. I do know that it's upstate somewhere. And a few hours' drive, actually. And with our recent merger with Omni Consumer Products, I don't think we'll be able to take the time to see Kevin. Not anytime soon, anyway.

It's sad, I know.

But I know he's happy. Why, we could hardly get the Prius to a stop before Kevin went bounding out of the car and went chasing after a flock of quarterly reports. I've never seen him so happy. Yes, they have quarterly reports roaming free, as well as endless hills of spreadsheets for Kevin to roam at his leisure. An abacus? Sure, Rachel, they have an abacus or whatever.

Look, you guys are asking a lot of questions, which I love! I love it. But we have a lot of work to do here and we can't spend all of our time asking about Kevin, who, quite frankly, all of you were complaining about not hardly a week ago, namely about how badly he smells and how he bit Theresa on the hand when she tried to shake the snow-globe on his desk.

"I've never heard of an accounting farm." Is that a question, Carl? It sounded more like a statement. What's an accounting farm? What did you tell Kevin's family? What's with that huge red stain in the parking lot? These are all wonderful questions and I will answer them soon, I promise. But, hey! How about we get a new accountant? Things have been pretty glum around here, haven't they? Why don't we take a look at the want-ads in the paper and see if we can find another accountant that we can fall in love with all over again? What do ya say, gang? I know... Kevin will be irreplaceable, but it's worth a shot. See? I'm forgetting about old what's-his-name already. Back to work, people! Terry, finish up those T.P.S. reports; I don't want to have to send you to a Merger and Acquisitions Farm.

Well, Excuse me, *Doctor,* But If Urine is So Sterile, Why Do I Feel Sick Every Time I Drink it?

Yes, a question if I may: before this goes any further I was just wondering if I could lob a query or two in your direction. Yes, yes, I know that there is a lot of ground to cover here but this should only take a second, honest.

First, I'm going to need you to leave your judgement at the door. We need complete objectivity if I'm going to get a straight answer here. Also, if you wouldn't mind getting the class to simmer down a bit; there's a lot of commotion going on here and I really need to hear your answer because it's important. No, they don't have to listen, although it would behoove them to do so, since I'm sure everyone has or will think about this at least once. And knowledge is power.

Now, I need to ask a question, and that is: Is urine sterile?

Short answer--yes. Thank you. I do appreciate your cooperation, I sincerely do. Now, you may be angry with me a bit, and I do apologize, because you have just been ensnared by my trap. You see, I *already know* that urine is sterile, as it is common knowledge. Heck, I learned about the sterility of urine alongside my ABC's. I did not want to deceive you, professor, but I had to set you up for my second question, which no one can seem to answer for me.

Trust me, if asking my one true question was as simple as just putting it out there and getting an informed answer, I would do it, as I have tried many times; friends, family, co-workers...none of them seem to be able to help me. Not only are they unable to help me, but they answer my question with other questions like, "What?" or "Huh?" or "Why? Why are you asking me this?" And last I checked, this was my life we were talking about and not some Abbot and Costello routine, so we can just go ahead and skip the humorous confusion and exasperation.

Sometimes I don't even get a response. It's true! Sometimes I just get this look of judgement and disgust from them and I don't deserve that. I truly don't. So, I like to coax people into my question. You know, start with broad strokes as if I'm just looking at the sky and pondering things. "Do you think there's an afterlife? When man first saw the ocean, did he ever wonder if the waves would stop? Is urine sterile, you think?" And after they answer "yes," WHAM! I ask them why I get sick every time I drink it. But still, the answer has eluded me.

So, please, *Doctor*, if urine is so sterile, why do I feel sick every time I drink it?

Yes! Good question! Okay, now we're getting somewhere. No, don't be shy, come at me with it. "Is the urine mine?" I appreciate the enthusiasm and the urge to engage. I personally was only speaking to the professor, but sure, if my classmates want to engage, that's fantastic! Yeah, let's get our hands dirty! Allow me to answer your question with a ratio figure: 70:30.

You see? You see right there! All that groaning and sounds of disgust, I'm *so* sick of hearing that; that sound makes me sicker than any "sterile" urine ever could. I went with 70:30 because I feared that even though this was supposed to be a mature group, you're no different. But alas, my eagerness to find the answer has overtaken whatever shame you want to throw upon me, so I'll shoot you straight, folks. It's 60:40.

What's that? Yes, in the back there. "Is it human urine?" Hmmm...I can't tell if you're setting me up for public mockery or not. Methinks you are, but I've never gotten this far before and my naïveté has gripped me something fierce. Okay, I'm going to go ahead and roll the dice and answer your question: Kind-of-mostly.

I knew it! I knew you guys wouldn't take this seriously! That's pretty much the only thing I do know anymore, since nobody is willing to answer my question. I know you're trying to make me feel ostracized, but it is *you* who should be feeling ashamed. Now, I'm going to leave, but I urge you to give my visit some thought, because I can almost guarantee at least eight of you will ponder the question once in your lives, as is our nature.

You Guys Remember When I Lost My Arm That One Time?

Yo yo yo! What's up, guys? Guess who's got himself an extra ticket to the Spacehog concert this coming Saturday? That's right: this guy right here! Now the only question being: which of you guys wants to go with me? You can go fisticuffs for it, you can bribe me with riches if you like; all of these options I will accept grandly. I expect no less than to be showered in either the graces of your humility or the physical spoils of your wanton eagerness. After all, this is Spacehog we're talking about here.

Now, before you all begin clamoring and clawing at each other, there is one small caveat I must mention briefly. Just real quick--you guys remember that time I lost my arm? Well, it--- what? What do you mean you don't remember?

Randy, hold on. I'll get back to the ticket in a minute. I find it kind of odd that you guys seemingly don't call to mind that one time I lost my arm. April 8th, 1994 (the same year that Spacehog formed, by the way)...taking a field trip to see the Liberty Bell...anyone? Anyone?

Randy, you're just saying you remembering so I will give you the ticket. I can see it in your eyes. No, I want you guys *recalling* this shit. Out of the four of you, two of you were there that fateful day. The school bus, speeding along Kelly Drive, the sunlight, the spring air, my arm sticking out the window to the hilt...

Nothing? Haha, ok, now, fellas. I am starting to feel kind of foolish, when it should be *you* feeling ashamed. It..hahaha...it was kind of a life-changing moment for me. But that's cool. It's not like, for instance, *Dave*, that after my arm snapped backwards like a rotted twig in a cold January wind and I started screaming and brought my stump back inside the bus and sprayed your face in my squirting arm-blood as the bus careened out of control and we crashed...no, I can see how you might have blocked that out. How very traumatic *for you*, Dave.

Guys, this wasn't a disposable fork or a grape that rolled under the couch. This was my fucking arm, ok? Randy! In a minute, for Chrissake!

How about the weeks following that incident? Did anyone wonder why the principal, Mr. Skiffington, was parading me around to various schools and holding assembly meetings to tell other kids not to do what I did? I was a wounded goat on tour, for crying out loud!

Maybe you're right. Maybe I am making too big a deal about this. All I wanted to say about the ticket was that, well, if you guys remembered *what happened* to my arm, I could just say that last week it happened again. Not *exactly* like before, but enough to pretty much just highlight, copy, paste; and whoever is going with me, I need you to drive. That's all.

Randy, what do you mean, "Nevermind"???

This Condolence Card Should Add Just the Right Amount of Sexual Tension

Hey, Karl. I just heard that Sally, Mr. Neuschwander's secretary, has been out for the past couple days because her favorite Aunt died. Is that true?

Sally, the petite, sexy red-head? Sally, the one with the contagious laughter? Sally, the one with tits to die for?

Sure, Karl, I'll sign the card. Yeah. It's a shame about her Aunt, I know. Tell you what, why don't you give me a couple minutes here and I'll get the card back to you? It's not every day that a sexy redheaded woman's favorite aunt dies. I'll be back in a few minutes with this.

I must be careful when choosing my words here. I've passed by her desk countless times, sometimes giving her a nod, but most of the time I just look at my feet and shuffle past her while I flop sweat. But this "dead aunt" thing... this could really parlay me from a pit-stained loser to a pillar of strength and sexuality in her life.

I wonder how much sexual tension you should have in a condolence card. Let's open up the card and see what we're dealing with here…

Oh, look, there's Karl's message right in the middle. I thought he was married. What's he doing taking the center of the card like that? "I'm so sorry for your loss." Geez, Karl, lighten up will you? You're not going to get Sally in bed that way being all mopey and sad. Sally wouldn't go for a guy like you anyway. I can't imagine her sitting there and listening to you recite some sad poem you wrote back in high school.

Wow, lots of guys signed this. Which, I mean, what was I expecting? It's Sally; of course there's going to be a lot of guys taking advantage of this opportunity. Oh, my god! Is that Gwen's signature there in the corner? I didn't know Gwen was a lesbian! That's super hot! Gwen, thanks for coming out to everyone, but I'm pretty sure Sally is straight.

I also see a lot of frowny faces, which totally ruins my strategy. I'm going to have to get more creative than I thought with this. It's going to have to be something sweet, sensitive, and sexual all at once. Something that says tenderly, "I'm here for you. I'm here for you and I have an erection."

...And I don't think a well-placed pun has ever NOT done that!

I wasn't planning to go nuclear on the competition, but this is Sally we're talking about here, and I think a little wordplay is totally legal at this juncture.

Psst! Hey, Karl! Real fast: how did Sally's Aunt die? Car accident? Seriously? That's perfect! No, just give me another minute, I'll be right back.

Dear Sally, if you ever need to talk about your Aunt, I am here for you. What do you say we go out to a bar and get **wrecked.**

It's almost not even fair. I wonder how many kids she'll want to have...

Hey, Karl. Here's the card. No, I sealed it. Nothing more needed to be said.

Welcome to Kmart Layaway, You Depress the Ever-Loving Shit Out of Me!

Hello, and welcome to Kmart's Holiday Layaway Program! My name is Jessica and you depress the shit out of me!

Before you show me what products most people can buy ten times over with whatever they may have in their wallets, allow me to first congratulate you on making the financially responsible decision to realize that you cannot properly provide for your children, but are still trying to keep that fact from them, at least for one magical morning. Kudos!

So let's see what items you can't afford to buy right now, but will treat as if it were a major purchase such as a car or a house. Oh, the Hasbro bundle package! That includes the Game of Life as well as Sorry! I *pray* you're trying to be this poetic on purpose, otherwise I am going to hit the wine extra hard tonight.

Honestly, you won't believe how much wine I

have to drink every night to erase the memory of people like you from my day!

I see you'll also be buying the "Three Howling Wolves," t-shirt in multiple sizes; a standard for poor trash such as yourself. Nothing howls of freedom quite like the beautiful majesty of paying for cotton t-shirts in nickels and dimes that were found between your black sofa cushions. I believe if you buy 4 of these you get a free NASCAR bumper sticker for your pickup truck that I am sure is filled with various blue tarps, sections of PVC pipe, and bungee cords that you never seem to use. No? Just stick with the three? Fair enough.

And what final item will we be making a down payment on tod... oh, c'mon, please, don't. You might think it's a good idea to do this, kind of a good motivator, like someone putting a gun to your head, but trust me, this won't end well. Don't put your Christmas tree on layaway. This job was already depressing enough before you put that fake tree on my counter. I think if I complain any more to my boyfriend about this job, he's going to start hitting me. Please take the tree off the counter. Just give up smoking menthols for one week and you can buy a real tree! Think of that! I know you probably like keeping your fake tree up in your living room until February, but with a real tree you don't even have to pack it back into a box, you can just leave it out by the curb a few days after Christmas. It's its own little miracle!

Alright, fine, have it your way. I will keep you items behind this counter until you make your final payment. But really, as soon as you turn your backs I'm putting this stuff back on the store shelves.

Bruce Merriweather: Lyrical Fact-Checker

BRUCE: Elton, come on in here, you son of a gun! How are ya?

ELTON: 'ello, Bruce. I'm well. I'm well.

BRUCE: Fantastic. Wonderful. Hey, listen, I don't need to tell you this, but you sir, are a hit-making machine!

ELTON: Well, thank you, I---

BRUCE: You're working on your fifth album with us, and I can tell already that it's going to be big.

ELTON: Do you really think so?

BRUCE: Big, Reggie, BIG!

ELTON: Please, you can call me Elton.

BRUCE: I'm sorry. Of course, of course. Elton. Mr. Elton John. Elton John, listen, I've been listening to the song we're going to release as a single.

ELTON: What song would that be, Bryce?

BRUCE: "Rocket Man." I have such a good feeling

about this song. You can just feel that it's going to be a hit. I know it. You know it. Hell, the people that haven't even heard it yet know it. And to call it "Rocket Man," shoot, are we talking about an Astronaut or your journey to the top of the charts, eh?

ELTON: Thank you, Bruce, but why exactly am I here?

BRUCE: Well, see, I've been listening to the song over and over again, because I love it so much, you see. And there's just a couple of lyrics I was wondering if you could help explain it to me, because it kind of throws me for a loop.

ELTON: Sure, alright, I hope you're not about to take the piss here, are you?

BRUCE: Oh, goodness no, Elton. And for anyone who is not British, they should know that "taking the piss" means to mock at the expense of others. No, no, no. There will be no piss-taking here, Elton. I was just hoping to clear up a couple of lyrics here.

ELTON: Alright…

BRUCE: Let me just say, again, how fantastic this song is. You got the man, the rocket, the loneliness therein, it all paints a wonderful portrait. But then we get to the bridge, where you say, "Mars ain't the kind of place to raise your kids. In fact, it's cold as hell. And there's no one there to raise them if you did."

ELTON: Yes, so?

BRUCE: Do…do you not hear how that sounds?

ELTON: Bruce, I'm sorry, I don't know what you're getting at here

BRUCE: It's okay, it's okay. Let's dissect it, shall we? Okay, first line: "Mars ain't the kind of place to raise your kids." Couldn't agree more. It should go without saying that with an atmosphere made mostly of carbon dioxide and is 100 times thinner than that of Earth's is not the ideal place to start a family. Of course you shouldn't be raising kids there. I would advise anyone against it. Now, if you're talking about maybe colonizing Mars and terraforming the planet, that's not really implied, and honestly that is science fiction stuff. We wouldn't see anything like that until at least 1989.

ELTON: Agreed.

BRUCE: Okay, next line: "In fact, it's cold as hell." So true it hurts! A summer day on Mars near the equator can get up to about room temperature, but once the sun sets, boy, the temperature plummets to minus 100 Fahrenheit. If that's not cold as hell, shoot, I don't know what is!

ELTON: What about near the poles?

BRUCE: Oh, the poles, even colder! I'm talking down to minus 195 degrees Fahrenheit. Isn't that nuts?? Who's raising children there? Not me, that's for sure!

ELTON: See, I had a feeling it would be colder near the poles because here on Earth the North Pole is really cold and Antarctica is, like, way down there…

BRUCE: Elton, you're brilliant. Good deductive reasoning, that's why you're such a talent. "But there is no one there to raise them if you did."

ELTON: Pardon?

BRUCE: That's the last part I want to question you about. "There's no one there to raise them if you did."

ELTON: (stammers)

BRUCE: You see, Elton, it just doesn't make sense. You're saying Mars isn't the kind of place to raise your kids, because there is no one there to raise them if you did raise them there.

ELTON: I don't follow…

BRUCE: Me neither! It's a puzzle, right?

(awkward silence)

ELTON: You see, Bernie, um, actually....

BRUCE: No, see, I'm gonna have to kind of stop you right there, because I talked to Bernie Taupin before talking with you, and although he helped with the melodies, he had nothing to do with the lyrics. Now, is there any way to change the lyrics so that they can be more...uh...palatable to the common radio listener?

ELTON: I don't...

BRUCE: Hey, between me you and the wall here, I think we both get it. I understand it. You're a genius, Elton, but maybe you could just dumb it down for the more pedestrian people out there, okay? We don't want you to blow their minds just yet, okay?

ELTON: I don't know, I suppose I just sang it once like that on the fly and it kind of stuck with the song, ya know?

BRUCE: Sure, sure. Of course. I'm not the talent; I'm just the fact-checker and quality assurance guy. It's my job to bring attention to these little things. In fact, right after talking with you I have to drive across town and meet with Pete Townhsend; apparently he is writing a musical about a deaf, dumb, and blind kid who plays pinball with...let me see here...(shuffling of papers) plays pinball with his... sense of smell?! Good God! Listen, Reginald, I gotta go take care of this thing, okay?

ELTON: A pinball wizard, eh? That sounds pretty-
--

BRUCE: Mr. John, if you could just worry about your own stuff for now. So, keep it, rewrite it, it's up to you. I just wanted to bring it to your attention. It's your choice, babe. Just remember, by your logic, if you rewrite it, it's not going to be easy, and there won't be anyone there to rewrite it if in fact you do rewrite it.

ELTON: What?

BRUCE: Exactly.

What is That Stuff in Your Ear and What Can We, As a Society, Do About It?

Okay, enough is enough. I can't stand to see you like this anymore. Heck, I don't even know you and I feel sorry for you. You feeling alright, man? You don't look alright. You seem off-balance, kinda got this herky-jerky way about you. Yeah, and you're digging pretty deep into that ear of yours. No, you weren't being very inconspicuous, there were a lot of us looking at you. It's safe to say we pegged you as schizophrenic, but you're white and you've got a briefcase so...

Hey, just calm down. Take it easy. It's going to be okay. Have a seat here. Breathe deep. Feeling better? Now, what have you got going on in that ear of yours and what can we, as a society, do about it?

I'm hearing a lot of opinions already and the

majority seem to think that you need to give the side of your head a good smack and dislodge whatever you got going on in there. This is, after all, a democracy we're living in, so what do you say? You wanna slap your head for us? Oooo, Jimmy here's got a safety pin! Not bad, Jimmy, but that's a little premature, don't you think?

Jimmy, I like where your head's at, but we're not at that point yet. Don't worry, buddy, there's a whole list of things we need to check off before we go jamming safety pins in your ear. After all, this is America; if we could land a man on the moon, then surely we can figure out whatever action you got going on in that ear canal of yours.

Personally, I'm going with wax buildup. Occam's Razor right? "Between two hypotheses, the one with fewer assumptions should be selected." Wax build-up: simple, straightforward, fixable. And as much as I hope it is a buildup of ear-grease, you shouldn't worry if that isn't the case. There are plenty more things we can do. Quick, does anyone here have an ear-plunger? That little blue thing with the bulbous end for suction? Anyone at all?

Come on, you telling me that between all of us here, we can't find a single ear syringe thingy? Oh, I'm sorry, did we not cure polio? That's right, Debra, we did, with good old-fashioned hard-work and determination. Jonas Salk was walking around, looking at all these crippled kids and he was like, "Well, I don't care for *this*," and BAM! Polio vaccine. So, shoot me straight: who here has an ear-plunger?

Betsy, yes! Betsy coming through in desperate times! Jonas Salk would be proud! You see what I'm talking about here? America! Heck yes! Ok, truth be told, Betsy's ear-thing is a little...used, so don't mind if I give it a little wipe on the sleeve....there we go! Ok, let's get us some wax!

...

...

...

Hmmm....you know what? I don't think this is working. It doesn't feel like I'm getting anything here. You feeling any better, buddy? Yeah, I didn't think so. But it's ok! It's ok. I want to take a look in there with a flashlight and see if we can make sense of this situation. We need to fully assess this state of affairs, but I want you to trust me, okay? Trust *us*. Listen: this country made Olestra, alright? All the taste of fat without the fat! Who else but us? Never-mind the anal leakage! Stop focusing on the negative, pal. We have an ear to rescue!

Okay, tilt your head to the side....Jimmy, do me a favor and stay close, alright?

...

...

...

Okay. (Puts flashlight down. Takes deep breath.) Okay, here's the sitch... (Turns flashlight back on, takes one more quick peak) Yeah. This may not be the most hopeful conclusion, but we do now have at least a definitive answer. And I can't help but think of the great Henry Ford who once said that is it not the size of the...oh, to hell with it. It's a bug; there's a fucking bug in your ear.

Wait! Everybody, calm down! Stop it! Get back here! Are we honestly going to run away from this problem? We're innovators! Do you think the inventor of the Snuggie would have stopped at his first roadblock? When he showed people his invention and they were like, "Yeah, it's a robe." Do you think he quit? Heck no, he didn't! And now look at him: a millionaire for inventing a robe, which was invented by people thousands of years ago! Think about that. Think about *that*. Now, surely, this is not the first time someone had a bug in their ear. It was probably all too-common in days of outdoor sleeping situations or back when beds were nothing more than piles of hay in a corner. The question is: are we going to capitalize on it (e.g. the Snuggie), or are we going to scatter back and claim it's impossible(e.g. the rest of the world?)

Good. I'm glad you feel that way. What a country we live in! Alright Jimmy, you still got that safety pin? Well, what the hell else do you want me to do? We have to do something! Guy's got a fucking bug in his ear. Personally, if it were me, I'd chop my own head off because that's the grossest thing I've ever seen and I once knew a kid who'd eat his own scabs, so there ya go. But if this guy wants to live… you still want to live, right, pal? God, how? But he does! He does, so let's see if we can do something. Let's brain-trust this bitch.

How big is the bug? Well, it's big enough for me to question living in a just world, but small enough to convince me we can do something about it. Good question, Gary. And it has antennae, if you must know. Now, what I'd like to do is stab the thing and keep it from rummaging around in there then maybe flush the corpse out with water or something. Guys, I think we can do this. Shit, we made Crystal Pepsi, didn't we? Didn't that shit blow your *mind* back then? All the taste of regular Pepsi but it looks like club soda.

The fuck was that about anyway? Well, it's over, that's for sure. Now, where were we? Right! The ear! Sorry, slipped my mind for a second.

I would like to go with the safety pin method, but I'm also getting curious about perhaps a fishhook approach. That way if I can get in there and stab it, it might also grip that little fella and we can pull him out. What you want to do with him after he gets pulled out is up to you, it's none of my business. But if you have a memory box, I think he would make a welcomed addition because this is shaping up to be a pretty rare morning, I must say!

Jimmy, can we crook that safety pin a bit and get this started? Jesus, I'm sweating. I don't think I've ever felt so alive. Ok, you ready, pal? Let's shine some light in there and....Ew!! Ew, it looked at me! Ew Ew Ewwwwwww! I'm out. I'm out, I can't do this. I don't care if you call me a coward, that's fine. This is the most disgusting thing I've ever seen. Call me a quitter too, I don't care. What do you expect from us? We invented the Flowbee for Christ's Sake. "What's a Flowbee?" Oh, fuck my uncle. You're beyond help. Good luck, pal! I gotta move to Canada.

I Interview Neil Clark Warren, Founder of EHarmony

Neil Clark Warren, welcome to your interview!
Thank you very much, Michael. How are you today?

I'm doing quite well. A little exhausted from Christmas decorating, but I'm sure I'm not alone.
Exhausted? I only see one string of colored lights plugged into the wall.

I know. Pretty, right?
Well, they're just lying on the floor…

I don't want to sound too crazy, Neil Clark Warren, but in actuality I've had this place decorated for Christmas since Halloween. But don't tell, okay? Don't tell anybody that.
Your secret's safe with me, Michael.

I knew I could trust you, Neil Clark Warren, founder of Eharmony. I imagine that your dating site is probably booming this time of year, what with the high rate of suicides in December and all.
Truthfully, the high rate of suicide in December is a myth. It is actually lowest in December. The highest suicide rates are in the spring and the fall.

Haha, c'mon Neil, what're you doing? You're

hurting my line of questioning here. I was just curious about how many people try your website in a last-ditch effort to feign off that gnawing hunger of seasonal suicide.

I certainly hope people aren't doing that, Michael. That sounds terrible! Our website has a very high success rate. In fact, we are responsible for over 600,000 marriages and counting!

Wow, that is a lot! And what percentage of those 600,000 marriages gracefully mature themselves into murder/suicides?

Michael, what's wrong? This doesn't sound like you. Your interviews are never this dark.

I'm sorry, Neil. It's this single living that's getting to me a bit. I guess I'm a little depressed over the nagging loneliness that gets more and more persistent with each day that passes.

Have you been meeting people or going out on any dates…?

Yeah, well, no, kinda… I mean, I got stood up for a date last week.
(sharp inhale) Michael, I'm sorry to hear that.

Yeah, I was pretty amped about it, but she never showed. Never answered her phone, nothing. I sat there at that Arby's booth for 2 hours like a dope.

That does sound odd. Did you do anything out of the

ordinary leading up to the date?

No! I played everything cool. I was funny and charming on the phone. I was relaxed. I asked her about her favorite sexual positions and whether or not her parents made a lot of money. And if she didn't answer, I left very polite voicemails where I breathed heavily into the phone for about 6 minutes. Standard stuff, really.

Michael, I can't tell if you're joking, ummm… maybe it was nothing on your end, maybe she got cold feet or something happened in her personal life and she didn't have the courage to tell you so she just never got back to you.

Do you think maybe she died? I'd feel so relieved if she were dead. Because, I mean, how else could a girl pass up on *this*, ya know?

Yeah…or maybe it just wasn't a good fit.

Hey! Speaking of good fits, I see that your website isn't just about matching up white single Christians anymore.

Yes, that is very true. Since we have over 20 million registered users, the eHarmony member base is an ethnically, racially, and religiously diverse group, and we are all looking to find that special someone.

Neil, I couldn't have said it better if I cut and pasted that from your website. Let's see what you got here: you got Jews, Blacks, Asians, Hispanics,

and people over 30. I had no idea that people over 30 were a minority.

Well, there are certain ideals and goals a person in their 30's has that someone in their 20's won't, you understand.

I suppose so. But maybe the next time I get pulled over by a cop I will ask him, "Is this because I'm over 30?"

...

I also understand that in 2008 you were ordered by the state of New Jersey to open your website to gay couples.

Yes, that is true, otherwise we would have lost all of our business in New Jersey.

I thought the homosexual community already had a dating site. It was called, "The Park After Midnight," Boom! C'mon, Neil! High-five.

I don't think that's very funny, Michael. That incident in 2008 was very volatile to our workforce. Many right-wing Christians were upset with us and threatened our lives on a daily basis.

Sounds pretty Christian to me.

I have said publicly that we should put up 10 million dollars and other companies should do the same so that we can figure out homosexuality.

Wow, that is an interesting, actual quote from

you, Neil. "Figure out homosexuality." Now, I don't have 10 million dollars, but I do have a Rubik's cube and I have been trying to figure this thing out for months. It's been boggling my mind day and night.

Oh, those things are easy to figure out.

You think so?

Yeah, just peel off the stickers and put them back together so that each side makes a solid color. That's how you solve a Rubik's cube.

Of course! How silly of me. Thank you very much, Neil. Do you think maybe I could join your website in the hopes of finding happiness?

Yes, yes of course you can, Michael!

One little caveat, um...I don't have any money.

Then no, I'm sorry, you can't find happiness.

Yeah, that's okay; I'm used to it. Neil Clark Warren, everyone.

Man, This Stripper Is All *Over* Me

Guys, guys! Check it! See that hot babe working the pole over there? That's Jocelyn and she *totally* digs me; she told me so. She said I am not like the other guys in here and she's right. I'm a sensitive guy. I'm a listener.

I'm sorry, Randy. Could you speak up? I said I am a listener, not a mind-reader. No? If you got something to say, just say it. Didn't think so.

Anyway, I was having a private dance with Jocelyn a few minutes ago and she was telling me about how all the other guys in here (including you knuckle-heads) are so ugly and don't really care about a woman's needs. Ergo, I am an attractive man who knows what a woman wants. Yes, Gary, she did say this while grinding against my junk and asking for the money up front. What's your point? Look, she knows it's a job, I know it's her job. But she was honestly happy to "finally have a hot guy to dance for," as she so eloquently put it. She said that only confident men wear green corduroys.

Guys, I think I'm in love.

Hey, did you know that you're supposed to tip the stripper? I'm sorry. I mean "dancer." Did you know you're supposed to tip the dancer *twice*? I thought I should give you a heads up on that. Yeah, Jocelyn told me. You're supposed to tip the dancer on the way into the "private dance" area, then again on the way out. You're also supposed to tip the heavy-set black guy manning the door who eyes you up the whole time. He's not just keeping the girls safe. He's keeping *you* safe as well.

Clyde, I don't see what's so funny about safety.

I never thought I would date a stri...private dancer. This is going to prove tough on my patience. I know it's kind of ironic to say it, but I don't think I want her taking her clothes off for other guys once we settle down together. I know it *sounds* hypocritical...? But that's just the way I feel...? And isn't that what part of love is about? Is overcoming odds and compromising? I don't see it as me making her quit so much as I am rescuing her from this place. It's like that romance movie starring Richard Gere, *An Officer and a Gentleman,* except that I am a toll booth operator.

I already have these cute nicknames picked out for her for when we are going to the antique store on weekends and buy cute little knickknacks----wow! Look at her work on that pole! Where was I?

Right. I could call her "Jocelot." You know, like "ocelot," but fashioned with her name. It's adorable. Or I could be like, "Hey, could you toss me the *T. V Guide?* Thanks a Joce-lot."

Yeah, you're right, Steve. Nobody reads *T. V Guide* anymore.

Personally, I think this is a done deal. She didn't tell me when her shift ends exactly, but I feel like I could walk up to her anytime and ask her out. You don't believe me, Randy? She likes me, she said so. I'll prove it. You want to bet? Fine! 50 bucks. Well, I don't have 50 bucks on me right now, not anymore. But you know I'm good for it.

Ask Me About My Grandcats

See that sticker on the bumper of my car? It says, "Ask me about my grandcats!" I applied it to my car with sincerity. Go ahead: Ask me about my grandcats!

Notice how the sticker is an actual sticker and not some fly-by-night magnet that can be applied and taken off on any philosophical whim. No, my sticker is permanent. Ask me about the cats!

I'm sure at first glance you might have presumed that my bumper sticker was a typo, but it's not. The silhouettes of the numerous cats next to the wording disprove your "misspelling" theory. No, this bumper sticker is the real deal.

If you're reading this sticker, then you must be behind me, stuck in traffic, trying to pass the time, I suppose. But there are no other stickers to read on the back of my 1986 Chevy Windsor. Why not get out of the car, give a rap on the driver's side window and heed the words of the sticker? Come on over. I won't bite!

Here's a little secret of the cat-trade: it is not too difficult to become a grandparent of cats.

They actually reproduce quite rapidly. Why, you could go through three generations of catdom in five years' time if you don't mind a little incestuous magic with your cat family. I got the sticker when I first became a cat grandparent over 12 years ago. At this point, to be honest, my sticker should say, "Ask me about my great-great-great-great-great-great-great Grandcats," but I don't think my bumper is wide enough to hold such a sustained message! Nyuk Nyuk!

And these aren't just cats, mind you. They're *grand*-cats, and I mean that in every sense of the word. Would you like to hear the reasoning? All you have to do is ask. All somebody has to do is ask!

My latest generation of cats seems to have been born without much motor skills. They tend to limp while they walk in concentric circles, but that only adds to their adorability and cutesy-wutesy ways! Also, their eyes are colorless.

Are you intrigued? Would you like to hear more? Come on over! Before the light turns green! You shan't regret it! Ask me about the grandcats!

This Relationship Was Much More Romantic When You Were In That Coma

It's an obvious truth that nobody wants to get nailed by an oncoming train, I know that. It was one of the saddest moments of my life when I heard the news that you were sitting unconscious in the hospital, and the doctors didn't have any idea when you would snap out of it, if at all. It was tragic, it really was.

But my love for you would not give up any inkling of hope for you; for us. Every day, every day for 8 months I came to the hospital to visit you, and held your limp hand, just hoping, praying for you to squeeze back, to let me know that we would be whole again. I missed your laugh, your stark sarcasm, and the apparent aloofness that you portrayed in order to cheer me up when I was feeling down. I did anything I could to see a small smirk to come across your face to give me just a little reminder of the happiness I could make for you.

And now, after 8 months, you're awake again.

And you're being a real bitch.

Listen, Honey, I've told you time and time again that with our budget, we can't go out every single night of the week. I'm working my ass off in order to provide us with a better life, but you just want to go ahead and blow it all on concerts, fine dining, fancy clothing, and exotic trips that I can't even go on because I have to work longer hours to pay for it. You used to have a little humility, but you've changed. Now you're all, "Gimme gimme gimme!" And worse yet, you don't even thank me.

Yes, you're right; we could all die tomorrow and everything would have been for naught, but you have to have faith that you're not going to die tomorrow, otherwise I won't be able to retire until I'm 106. Just take it easy, alright? I'm sorry about the coma, I am. However, we have to go on as it was before. I can't stand your temper-trantrums when you don't get what you want, calling me a lousy person and a terrible provider. It's ridiculous and humiliating, especially when you do it in public. I don't deserve that.

Sometimes at night, before I fall asleep for 4 hours between my 2 jobs, I listen to your horrendous snoring, and I remember how peaceful and romantic your coma days were. It was a beautiful gesture when I came in your room

with fresh flowers every other day, enthusiastic
that the smell would arouse your awakening, and
how everyone watched with a tearful eye as I
held your hand and told you about my day, about
the beautiful things going on in the world that
you needed to see. Oh, how those nurses wanted
to bang me! But I didn't, I focused on you, and this
is what I get.

If Craig T. Nelson Were My Uncle, I Think I'd Be Terrified Pretty Much All of the Time

God, I can't even imagine it. Well, I can *kind* of imagine it, but it's not pleasant. I don't even think I'd be able to write this article because I would constantly be looking over my shoulder if I were the nephew of Prime Time Emmy winner and Golden Globe Nominated actor Craig T. Nelson.

I wish to continue my statements after admitting that I actually have no familial relation to Craig T. Nelson (thank goodness!) I also have no social relationship with Mr. Nelson. Mr. T. Nelson does not know that I exist and for that I am thankful because my life is hard enough as it is.

Standing at an unconscionable 6'4", many people know Craig T. Nelson most recently as the lovable patriarchal figure from NBC's *Parenthood*, where he played Zeek Braverman, a tough but caring Vietnam Vet who loves his family, but I know better. I first remember Craig T. Nelson as the scary-looking guy from *Poltergeist 2: The Other Side.*

He drank the worm!

First, a little background: If you've seen the movie then I needn't remind you of the scene, but for those who are unscarred by the existence of Craig T. Nelson, I will tell you about it. In *Poltergeist 2: The Other Side*, Craig plays Steve Freeling, a father whose family is going through some tough times because an unrepentant demon is trying to take over the soul of his young daughter, played by Heather O'Rourke. Understandably, due to the stress of this, Steve decides one night to hit the bottle to take the edge off.

Craig T. Nelson chooses a bottle of tequila as his drink of choice for this brief little escape from the horrors of his victimized family. At the bottom of the bottle was a worm, which I hear is not uncommon, so I'm not going to hold it against him. If Craig T. wants to drink the worm, then Craig T. can drink the worm. Of course, I will be judging Uncle Craig T. for drinking nearly an entire bottle of the stuff. An entire bottle! That's a terribly irresponsible thing to do even if your daughter is *not* being stalked by an evil entity. I'm just saying, kids do not care if you're hungover the next day; they will not sympathize with your plight.

So, Craig drinks the worm, but little did he

know that the worm he ingested was actually an embodiment of the demon that was stalking the family! There are days and there are days. So, Craig T. gets super-scary when he gets all evil on the family and just when you thought it couldn't get any worse, the worm *grew* inside of Craig T. until eventually Mr. Nelson upheaved a half-digested, half-born, half-dead cult leader which squirmed across the bedroom floor and smiled at Craig T. with a mouth full of adult teeth before shimmying out the door only to gain strength and terrorize his family even harder at a later date.

My first thought when I saw the scene at age 6 was, "God, I really hope Craig T. Nelson is not my uncle," which I have heard is a common thought among children when first watching *Poltergeist II: The Other Side*. And don't try to tell me that after he swallowed the worm in *Poltergeist II*, even his real nieces and nephews didn't disown him entirely; and with just cause. He was absolutely terrifying!

I asked my parents if we were related to Craig T. Nelson because if we were, I was going to have to cut out a lot of the riff-raff in my own life: the video games, the sugary snacks, the complaining, the sarcastic remarks…if my uncle was Craig T. Nelson, I don't think he'd put up with any of that shit; not him nor the possible puke baby/old man he may have lurking around in his man-womb.

My parents said no, we weren't related to Mr. Nelson and I took a sigh of relief. But I thought about it often, especially as Craig T. Nelson kept popping up in my life through the television. In 1989, I was convinced that he played Vigo the Carpathian in *Ghostbusters 2*, even though he didn't. At the time, you couldn't convince me otherwise. Vigo and Craig were both tall, big-faced men with a shiny veneered forehead that held fast to a mane of hair in the back of their skulls. When my friends and I would watch the movie, at the first appearance of the Vigo painting, I would pause the VCR and say, "You see that guy? That guy is *not* my uncle." And then I would resume the video. I would say it not so much to convince my friends, but more to convince myself; you know how kids are.

Even though the Ghostbusters vanquished Vigo, I knew all too well that when it came to Craig T. Nelson: Death is but a door. Time is but a window. He will be back.

And as the door shut on Craig T's (non) appearance in *Ghostbusters 2*, the window that is the ABC sitcom *Coach* opened for Craig T. Nelson where his fear-mongering forehead burst into our living room every Monday night. I don't know why it was called a "situation *comedy*" if it was starring the guy who got shitfaced, puked up a goddamn demon, and terrorized his poor, haunted family-- but that's network television for you.

And if I were his nephew, I would probably know that Mr. Nelson made his start in a comedy troupe called The Groundlings with Barry Levinson, the director of *Rain Man*. Craig would probably drop in those nuggets of information every time he came over for fireworks and hamburgers during the fourth of July. But I'd be persistent with my ignorance. "You're not fooling me, Uncle Craig T!" That's what I'd scream from behind the couch. "Dad, hide the Mezcal!"

Even though *Coach* aired for 9 seasons, those 199 episodes failed to remedy the paralyzing fear that those 39 seconds of demon-regurgitation in *Poltergeist II* caused. Now, I'm not saying that I don't have a family because I worry that I might be related to Craig T. Nelson, but I'd be lying if I said it isn't a significant factor.

What galvanizes the fear even more is the recent realization that even if Craig T. dies before me (as all uncles should), *Poltergeist II* has taught me that he can still be effective in our material world. So that began a long streak of sleepless nights that probably shaved years off of my life.

But now I know what I have to do. I have to use the knowledge that *Poltergeist II* bestowed upon me and use it against (Uncle?) Craig T. Nelson. In the movie, the Freeling family befriended an American Indian spirit guide named Taylor who helped identify and battle the demon who was terrorizing them. That's what I need to do: befriend an American Indian.

Unfortunately, in this country, I've seen more three-legged ballerinas than I have seen Native Americans, so I needed to conduct some research. I first looked up the man who played Taylor in *Poltergeist II*, but it turns out he died in 1987, just a year after *Poltergeist II* came out. Great, that's just my luck. I'm so screwed.

Well, what other Native Americans do I know of? There was the character Danny Lightfoot on Nickelodeon's hit western sitcom *Hey, Dude*. Maybe he can help. Well, it looks like Danny Lightfoot was played by a guy named Joe Torres. That name doesn't sound too American Indian-y. And, of course, it looks like *Hey, Dude* was his one and only role before he disappeared into obscurity after the show's cancellation in 1991. Christ, I can't get a break.

Joe Torres, if you're out there somewhere, I could really use your help. What I need for you to do is set up a tent in the Arizona boonies where we will take off our shirts and smear each other with war paint. Then we'll sit around the fire and I will breathe in some smoke and go on a spirit quest to combat my fear of Craig T. Nelson.

Yes, I am willing to take my shirt off for this endeavor; that's how cereal I am about this. And no, Joe, you don't have to apply the war paint to my chest if you don't want to. But I will need to call you Danny Lightfoot and you will have to give me some Native American wisdom before I battle the fear of Uncle Craig T. Nelson. Just let me know when you would like to do this, but we must act soon because I've put my life on hold for a long, long time due to this.

Thank you, Danny Lightfoot. I'll bring the tequila.

Looks Like That Dim-Witted Boy From up the Street is Discovering the Hornet's Nest Out Front

Hey. Hey, Mary. Take a look at this. Come here. Over by the window. See there? It looks like that dim-witted Baderman boy from up the block is about to discover that hornet's nest out front. Yeah, I know. I was *just* about to take care of that nest too, but now I think I should let this situation run its natural progression. No, no, you're right. I should warn him. Of course I will. *Of course.*

Hey, boy. Be careful there. Those hornets will sting you.

Stay away from that nest.

Gah, Mary, he isn't listening. What can I say, the boy is *dense.* His whole family, really. They aren't playing with a full bag of jacks, if you know what I mean. I went to High School with his father and I remember him snorting Pixie Sticks in our senior year. This kid never had a chance. Ten dollars--I'll bet you 10 dollars that peanut-headed evolutionary cul-de-sac out there thinks there's honey in that nest. You want a piece of that action? Hey, you remember last winter when he went door to door to see if we wanted our sidewalk salted? And I looked down and saw he had a bag of Morton's friggin' table salt in his hand?

Wait, shhh! He's getting a stick. Ha, even the stick is short, it's like, 6 inches long. Oh, god, this is going to be great! I had a feeling about today, Mary. Didn't I tell you when I woke up? I stretched out my arms and I just *knew* something magnificent was going to happen. And you thought this was going to be just another dull Saturday. Well, allow me to present to you Timmy Baderman: the scourge of rational thinking and suburban boredom.

Oh, god, look at him get near that nest. He better close his mouth lest a hornet flutters in that slack-jawed mouth of his.

Hey, do we have any lemonade? This show would go really great with some lemonade. Yeah, the pink lemonade is fine, I don't care. Just hurry back, because shit is about to go *down.*

You closed the other windows, right?

The Original Hooters

Oh, man! Did you *ever* miss out on the greatest business trip in the history of Gus's Tile Mart. I usually don't go to the Bathroom Tile and Grout Symposium; I'm kind of ahead of the curve in all things grout and tile, but guess where they held it this year? Clearwater, Florida, that's where!

Flo-Ride-Ah!

You'd think the highlight of the weekend might have been the latest innovations in silicone grout or the sneak peek into next year's splash tile color combos, but you'd be wrong. Dead wrong. Do you have *any* idea what's in Clearwater? Phillies spring training? Yes. They have that there. But guess what else. Guess, guess, guess.

Wrong, wrong, wrong.

I can't believe I have to tell you this. You are a *guy,* yes? Fine, I'll tell you: They have a Hooters down there. Oh, good. You've heard of it. God, for a second there I thought I was talking to a homo. Listen: not only do they have a Hooters in Clearwater, but they have *the* Hooters. The original. The authentic Hooters. The prototype that started it all. The Alpha Hooters, as it were. I was going to be sitting inside the very Hooters that begat a revolution of large-breasted women serving beer and chicken fingers. Imagine!

Shoot, I called for reservations before I even booked my flight! I called them up and asked for a table for Saturday night and this hot chick (you could tell she was hot) asked, "Okay, honey. Would you like to sit in a booth or out on the patio...?"

And I was like, "OMG, you guys have a patio??" You could tell Hooters definitely ruled the roost in Clearwater. This was going to be the best Bathroom Tile and Grout Symposium since they held it in South Carolina and I bought those sparklers and snuck them across state lines.

I booked a patio table for four because I was going to assemble a good crew for Saturday night. I decided to get the "bad boys" of Grout and Tile: Franky "Bounce-Bounce" Campini, Larry "Sniffles" Neuschwander, and Barry Breen, but everybody just knows him as, "The Claw;" you know, because of the eczema.

The four of us ditched the 2-hour synthetic grout lecture so we could tailgate at the Hooters parking lot. Nothing like a little pre-gaming to get your night at Hooters off to a great start! We got a great spot so we could wolf-whistle the Hooters girls as they came up on shift-change and we drank sooooo many Bud Lights, it was *ridiculous*. Frankie had to call his wife at one point, so we called him a fag and high-fived each other. *So much fun.*

As we approached the front door of the Mecca Hooters, the doors burst opened and we were greeted by 4 really pretty girls with big smiles and they said, "Hi, welcome to Hooters!" And I got so excited I started smacking myself on the top of my head and began howling like a wolf, because I knew the chicken tenders were going to be out of this world! Hooters is known for their chicken tenders. Larry put one hand over his heart and mimicked having a heart attack because these girls were so beautiful. We basically fell over each other in laughter and high-fives.

I'm sure the original Hooters has seen some pretty crazy times since its inception in 1983, but I don't think they were ready to handle the four chuckleheads of Grout and Tile, no sir!

After stepping inside, another pretty girl came over and seated us. She was also smiling really wide, so I assumed she just had some chicken tenders. (I hear Hooters girls eat for free.) As we were trying to decide what to get to drink, Frankie mentioned that there were no prices next to some of the items, like alcohol. I corrected him by saying, "What are you doing looking for prices on a menu? Did you see the gozangas on that girl?" Then I began slamming my palm on the table. "Hummina hummina hummina!"

It was intimidating to be in the presence of such history. The walls were covered top to bottom of photos of famous celebrities who have visited over its 35 year history: Justin Bieber, Fred Durst, Spencer Pratt, Jose Canseco, and the like.

I told the waitress I would love to get a photo with her after I ate my chicken tenders, but it was hard to speak with my tongue rolled out all the way to the end of the table. She said, "You're funny!" And I was like, oh my god, this is the best night of my life!

The Claw ordered a cheeseburger except it was called the "More Than A Mouthful Burger," and when he ordered it he said he'd have the, "More Than a Mouthful, so to speak." And we all were like, Oh, my god, Barry! You sly boots! And then we all laughed, including the waitress, because it was just *too* funny.

High-fives. Guffaws.

Everybody was having such a great time. It

was so awesome.

That is, until someone (Bounce-Bounce?) noticed that the pitcher of beer we ordered had this large, frozen rod in the middle of it. The waitress said it was attached to the pitcher and kept the beer cold. Then the guy was like, "but it's taking up all this space where we could fit more beer in here." I wasn't there for this exchange, as I was perusing the Hooters store and stocking up on Original Hooters merchandise: tee-shirts, polos, coffee mugs, shot glasses, cooking aprons, magnets, hoodies, and art prints.

Lexi (who also said I was funny!) was one of the girls who opened the door for us and she was helping me pick out some of the stuff and recommended that I buy at least 2 of everything so that I can give them as gifts as well as keep one for myself. And I was like, "Yes, my mom would love this boobzie koozie. It's like a beer koozie, but it's got hooters boobs on it. Oh, she's just going to *die* when she sees this. Good idea, Lexi."

Lexi was by far the best Hooters girl in the world. It's no wonder she was working at the original restaurant. I asked her if I could get a photo with her and our waitress. I said I would pay any amount because my friends are not going to believe me when I tell them that you two girls thought I was funny. And then guess what happened: Lexi laughed again. Oh, it was like taking candy from a baby, that's how charming I was being that night. It wasn't even fair, to be honest with you.

However, the night ended abruptly when Barry's eczema claw grazed the waitress's shoulder. Barry assured her that he wasn't contagious and that his hand was the only part of his body that looked like that, "If you know what I mean."

Then the manager came over and asked us to pay our bill and leave. I pleaded with the manager to let me purchase my Hooters gear and get a photo of Lexi, Sasha, and I before we leave. He said I could pay for my merchandise but that was it. I thanked him.

I thanked him because even though it was a relatively short visit, I was able to see and experience things I could have never imagined in a thousand nods. And I know that the staff at the Original Hooters will be talking about us for *years*, because our visit was so epic. You guys gotta believe me: they thought I was funny! Honest. Truly.

No, Wait-- NOW is the Best Time to Buy a Kia!

Just when you thought the time couldn't get any better to buy a new Kia, you have arrived at this moment. Now, more than ever, is it the perfect time to put yourself behind the wheel of a brand new Kia, here at Kia of Westchester and Kia of Coatesville.

I know we were advertising last month that the year-end factory blowout sale was *the* time to buy a new Kia, but that was untrue. And also, back in November when we offered one penny over invoice, we said that prices couldn't go any lower than that, but guess what? It was a lie! We were lying so hard, because you, my friend, have yet to strap yourself into a new Kia.

You're a savvy consumer; we can see that now. You waited. You bided your time and held fast, sitting idly by while we tempted you with half-hearted fallacies of once-in-a-lifetime savings. And this is the sale you've been waiting for.

Seriously, prices won't get any lower than this. I'm just the voice-over guy, but from what I hear at the dealership, it's that the owner, Jim Sipala, has gone off his nut and is offering zero percent APR financing as well as $3,000 for any kind of trade-in that you can make to the lot.

Seriously—any kind of trade-in! You got an old clunker that is just taking up space in the driveway? Is it missing some parts? A battery? Windshield wipers? An engine? Push it on down to Kia of Westchester or Kia of Coatesville and Jim will hand you $3,000 toward your new Kia.

You still use a horse and carriage to get around? Trot on down to visit Jim! He'll compliment your monocle and stovetop hat, all while handing you $3,000 dollars. But the horse is dead, you say? No problem! Simply bring in a hoof to Jim. He trusts you! Three grand for a hoof—guaranteed.

Look, once the higher-ups realize what Jim is up to, they're going to toss him in the loony bin. No joke! Jim is going to be wearing a straight-jacket because he *wants* to go out of business; that's how faithful he is to Kia automobiles. He is willing to take a heavy loss on each car that is driven off the lot. "Why," you ask? Because he's passionate. He believes in the Kia, as should you.

If Ghandi were alive today, he wouldn't be preaching non-violent protest, he'd be standing next to Jim at Kia of Coatesville or Kia of

Westchester and handing you the keys to your new Kia. He'd be like, "Be the change you want to see in the world...here at Kia of Coatesville or Kia of Westchester." So what are you waiting for??

Jim's bosses are nearing his dealership, fists raised and ready to storm the lot. Jim will be tossing keys out to every person within range, until finally, Jim will be overtaken by Kia stockholders. He will be kicked in the face by wing-tipped shoes worn by bald old men who don't see Jim's vision of you driving a new Kia. They will stomp him, they will spit on him, they will humiliate him in front of his family. He will be beaten within an inch of his life and will be given one final chance to repent this *ridiculous* sale of Kia automobiles. But he won't. He's literally dying to see you in a New Kia. On his last breath, he will see you drive off his lot in a brand new Kia. You will give a friendly honk of the horn and he will smile and wink at you as he parts from his mortal coil. Don't let Jim die in vain. Get yourself into a new Kia.

...

...

...

Okay, I know we said that at the beginning of this advertisement that it was the best time to buy a new Kia, but that was simply untrue. NOW is the best time to buy a new Kia—literally right this second is the best time to buy. No, wait, you missed it. Now…right…now! Buy! Shit, you missed it. NOW!

The Obvious Logistical Nightmare of Making Smurf Porn

Ok, places, people! It's been a long day and I want to get this scene in before we go home for the evening. But I want us to stay focused because this is a crucial scene. Gary, you want to make sure that people are standing in the appropriate spots? Has anyone seen Smurfette?

Sebastian, just hold tight for a minute while we find Smurfette, okay? I know it's hot under the lights, but you're a vital part of this scene. Gary, would you mind going to the dressing room to find Smurfette? I think she's still putting on the body paint.

Sebastian, please quit fluffing yourself. You're going to rub all the paint off and we'll have to reapply it before the scene starts. I know it's taking a while, but be patient. Be patient and hard. You see how the paint is rubbing off? Come on, Sebastian. You're Brainy Smurf! You're supposed to know this stuff. Hey, I wanted to use Krylon spray paint for the shafts, but noooooo! Your union reps put an end to that right quick. I'm just saying, if we used Krylon, you could fluff yourself for hours with only minor consequences, that's all.

In fact, Sebastian, why don't you go over to the catering table and get some of those blueberries up in you. I know it's probably impossible to turn your sperm blue, but it's worth a shot. Worst-case scenario: we'll turn it blue in post. Maybe add some glitter too, I'm not sure. After all, you are a magical Smurf. Plus, you're starting to smear from the hot lights.

Actually, Sebastian, while I have you for a minute, I'd like to talk to you about something. Do remember back in '94 when you starred in *Teenage Mutant Ninja Turtles: Secret of the Splooge*? You had that scene with April O'Neil and right at the moment you climaxed you yelled, "Cowa**cum**ba"? That made you a legend. Instantly. Sabby, I'm looking for that same type of magic for this scene with Smurfette. I know it's asking a lot, but I'm confident you can do it. I won't smother you with notes, but I'll trust your expertise to guide you with what to say when you Blam. Good talk, Sebastian.

Gary, where is Smurfette?? Ah, there she... (sigh) Gary, a word?

Why the hell is Smurfette purple? She looks like Grimace from the McDonald's Gang! Tell me,

Gary: are we making McDonald's porn? No! Not this month we aren't!

Gary, are you colorblind? You're colorblind, aren't you? Oh, fuck me running, this is just great! Well, if they were out of the color blue, why didn't you just call me? Look, if they're out of blue, just go back to Michael's Arts and Crafts and get some yellow and green. Didn't think of that, did you? Unfortunately, we don't have the money for it.

Take a gander at that gigantic papier-mâché Gargamel dick. Does it look like we have any money left in the budget for more body paint? I think not, Gary! Why? Because Smurfette was created by Gargamel, duh! That's why she's blowing him in this scene. Wouldn't you like to go down on your Creator? I know I certainly would.

It's not like this is the production of a lifetime and you're lucky enough to be working for a director who actually gives a shit about the source material. No, let's just slap each other silly with blue paint and have a free-for-all. Well, not today. Not with this director, no sir!

Gary, here's 40 bucks of my own money. Go down to Michael's Arts & Crafts and get all the green and yellow you can carry. The studio will reimburse me once this movie becomes an international sensation, guaranteed. No, don't return the purple; we'll save that for the McDonald's film next month.

Okay, I don't think we can do any more for the day. That's a wrap, people! Sebastian, you may fluff yourself to completion. We'll see you tomorrow.

I'd Like to Return This Baby in a Jar, Please

Good afternoon, Miss. If you don't mind, I'd like to return this purchase I made a couple weeks back. Yes, as a matter of fact, it *is* concerning the baby in this jar. Good eye! Very astute.

I don't know if you remember me or not, but I came in here a couple weeks back looking for something to really give my apartment that extra, lucrative, sexy sense of flair I felt was necessary as a young professional. Some people thought a pricey piece of local art would do the trick. Others suggested a fancy new flat-screen television would give the message that I was an up-and-comer, but I knew what would do the trick and I was fortunate enough to see your billboard ad while driving to my new job. It was kismet.

The moment I walked into this store I knew I was in good hands. Your greeter was extremely friendly and well-mannered, making me feel entirely welcomed and unjudged with regards to my purchase. I tried to talk to my friends about buying a pickled baby in a decorative jar and they always responded with that typical judgmental tone, "You want a *baby?* In a *jar*??"

But let me just say how refreshing it was to walk into your store and see a pretty young woman with a vibrant smile exclaim cheerfully, "Welcome to Baby in a Jar!" Surely, this was the store to fulfill all of my jarred baby needs. Your manager, Mr. Black, must be very proud.

Your sales staff embraced my decision to buy a baby in a jar with fascinating ease. Not only did they understand my need for such an item, they sat down with me and we discussed the color of the formaldehyde that would match my décor, as well as style of jar. Did you know how many different styles of jars there are? There's the Boston Round, The French Square, The Hex, and The Wide Mouth Packer just to name a few. I don't think you really appreciate all the different styles and modes of jars there are until you try to pack a dead fetus in there. Your staff was very patient with me and understanding of my feelings of being overwhelmed with your wide array of choices.

I'd like to also thank your staff for the professional manner not with just how they treated me, but with how gently they treated the jar-baby himself..? Herself? (snaps fingers) *Itself.* I've heard these little guys referred to as "pickled punks" or "Stillbies," but you would never guess these things weren't still alive. I was taught not to grab the baby in the jar by the top lid, but to cradle the jar as if it were a baby sans jar. Sans formaldehyde. Sans lack of pulse. As you can see, I am still doing that, cradling this lil guy in my arms as I speak to you. I know I don't need to be bobbing it up and down in a soothing motion; I know that. It's just my natural paternal instincts kicking in, you understand.

In the end, I went with an orange-tinted crystal goblet that would match the center-piece of my living room which is *La Reverie* by Renoir; framed reproduction, no big deal.

I'm tellin' ya, this pickled little punk really tied the room together.

I named him Bertram, hoping that it would be a funny little anecdote to tell guests. They would marvel at Bertram and how well he goes along with my Renoir and I would explain that you never hear of people named Bertram anymore. Then I would tap playfully on the goblet and go, "I wonder why." Oh, how we'd chuckle! We'd chuckle until our sides hurt, yes we would!

Clearly, you can see the potential.

I am saddened to say, Miss, that none of this

happened. In fact, quite the opposite. I should have taken my friends' judgmental tone to heart when they heard of just the *idea* of my purchase, but for them to see Bertram actually floating in that goblet right there in my living room, well, there was no chuckling. In fact, what's the opposite of chuckling? "Stern consternation"? Yes, I'd go with that.

It was not an easy decision to make, the purchase of the baby in the jar nor its subsequent return to this store, but it wasn't just my sense of style that people were criticizing. I understand if you might not like my choices concerning the layout of my bachelor pad or the color scheme I've chosen, but thanks to Bertram's prominent placement in the living room, people asked me, "What kind of a *person* are you?" And frankly, it hurt. Especially if the person who said it was a potential lover or my mother. Oh, how it stung!

Frankly, this is not about the $49.95. This is about giving Bertram a second chance at a better, more inclusive home than the one he was subjected to with me. No, I do not have a receipt. I didn't think it would be a problem. Sorry, I'm kind of scratching my head here. You are aware that you guys are the only store in this town--- well, in this *country* as far as I know that sells babies in decorative jars, yes? No, that's ok. That's fine. I will respect your store's policy. I'm not going to raise a fuss.

I guess since I can't get rid of Bertram by any legal means, I could always leave him out front of a firehouse and drive off before anyone sees me. Ok, thank you for your time. If –no– *when* people finally catch up to the aesthetic pleasure of your product, I will see you again; that's a promise, baby.

Thanks for the Hospitality

Dear William and Penelope,

I would like to sincerely thank you for opening your heart and your home to me while you were away on vacation. It has meant the world to me that I have such loving and caring friends who will treat me as a member of their own family. It has reawakened a level of trust with people that I thought I had lost long ago. I owe my renewed faith in humanity to you. Kudos!

I am sorry that I could not be there to welcome you back into your home, but you have more than likely shuffled through your front door, ready to unpack your bags, took a look around your humble abode and found this note hanging peacefully on your refrigerator.

And you are probably looking for some kind of explanation(s).

First, I do apologize wholeheartedly for the shaving crumbs I left in the bathroom sink. That was a happenstance of the morning rush I found myself in while getting ready today. I was terribly behind schedule to start my new life and didn't want to be a minute later than I already was. It was awfully inexcusable for me to take advantage of your house that way; to figure that someone (besides me) will clean up my mess. I mean, what am I, 2 years old? Puh-lease!

Next, you're probably wondering about the living room windows that were smashed in with a brick that was tied to another brick. That was the fault of my huffing buddy Lazlo. He can be a good guy sometimes and when I told him where I was staying, he didn't hesitate to come on over. Now, as far as the bricks are concerned...Lazlo doesn't have a cell phone; he has a pager. So when he needs to alert someone that he is at his destination, he simply fires a brick through the appropriate window.

I know, right? Who uses pagers anymore?

But as far as the brick that was tied to another brick: Lazlo told me that one brick carried the announcement of his arrival, while the one it was tied to was used simply to make the living room window yield to the message's demands. I know, I know. I told Lazlo that only one brick needed to be thrown, as it would be able to handle the burden of multi-tasking both the dropping of the window as well as delivering the prudent message. He has since promised that he would only throw one brick the next time he comes to your house. I apologize on his behalf.

The master bedroom may appear to show signs of a terrible struggle and I want to let you know right now that no one was harmed (in your bedroom). In our search for some decent airplane model glue in which to huff, we came to Penelope's armoire and soon spent the better part of an hour trying on her tiny shirts and "hulking out" numerous times before finally calling an escort service.

It's important to note here that there is a difference between "blood spatter" and when someone says "blood spLatter." "Spatter" is when it comes out in drops. "Splatter" is when it comes out in huge splashes.

So when you walk into the living room, William, you should say, "Penelope! There is blood spatter all over the walls and across our framed family photos!"

And Penelope, you should say, "Not just that, but William, look at this! There is blood splattered all over our family quilt!"

Do you notice the difference? Well, you'll see what I mean. Please use these words in proper accordance to the situation. The way people interchange these two words… It's an ignorance that really grinds my gears. Sorry, I was an English Major.

Lastly, in all the time it took to write you this letter, you would think I'd at least clean up the blood spatter. That is a wonderfully valid point to raise, but allow me to counter that point with a question: do you see the body of a soulless, bloodless prostitute anywhere? Please at least garner all the knowledge of a certain situation before you make any rash assumptions and look like a real jerk.

Again, thank you so much for your hospitality and grace that you have shown me by allowing me to stay here for the night. And thanks to the close proximity of your home near the courthouse, I was able to make my court-date on time.

Signed,

Michael Timothy

Ps.

If you insist on calling the police, please do so quietly, as Lazlo is probably around there somewhere, sleeping it off.

If My Boss, Mr. Shirley, Gave the Eulogy at My Funeral

(Long, somber whistle) What a sad day. I can't believe I'm up here in front of you folks this morning. How tragic, to lose a guy like Mike. For those of you who don't know, I am Mr. Shirley. I am--sorry, *was* Mike's boss over at Wexlar Family Plastic Sheeting. We offer competitive pricing for all of your product overwrapping needs. Wexlar Plastic Wrap: We Wrap the World!

I don't know how many of us saw this coming; I certainly didn't. Always showed up on time with an eagerness to cut some plastic film to the specific size requested by the customer; guy was a machine! Well, machine operator, to be more specific.

And not only was he a dedicated machine operator, he was a pleasure to be around. He showed up every day. Not only that, but he showed up every day *on time.* I know my own son, who happens to be Mike's supervisor, could learn a lesson or two from him.

What a loss this has been not just for Michael's family but for the family of Wexlar Plastic Film Slitting and Sheeting. We are going to miss Michael dearly. Especially next week when we start doing inventory. Oh, this loss hurts. It hurts bad! This death is tragic, as tragic as this year's inventory is going to be without Michael.

Michael's greatest strength as an employee, son, friend, and person in general, I think, was his ability to quickly and accurately fill out a T.P.S. Report. Man, could that guy fill out a T.P.S. Report! You gave that kid a T.P.S. Report, he filled it out, oh yes! I knew that as soon as I handed Michael a thick file of reports, they would all be diligently filled out and handed back to me in no time.

What remains a mystery for me, however, is where he could have put the T.P.S. Reports for the month of May. I've looked all over and cannot seem to find them. You're probably thinking, "Look in the filing cabinet, Mr. Shirley." Sure. I hear that a lot, but the May TPS Reports are not there! I can't believe it myself! January, February, March, April...all there, all accounted for, but not May. Michael, you died in a shroud of mystery.

And I don't think any of us saw this coming: Michael's death, the missing May reports, the topsy-turvy cluster-screw that will be this year's inventory…it's all come as such a shock. There are still so many unanswered questions that we must face as survivors of Michael. For instance, was Michael aware of his condition? If so, why didn't he take the necessary steps to seek treatment? And finally, most importantly, do you think he would have used a sick day or a vacation day on the day he died?

It's not as easy an answer as one might think. Listen, Michael died on a Thursday, right? But he left work early on Wednesday because he wasn't feeling well. He left at 11:00am on Wednesday and even though I shouldn't have, I only charged him half a sick day. Yes, he did leave before his half-hour lunch break, but he left in such a hurry it must have been an emergency. Of course, Payroll was really putting my balls in a vice and try to get me to charge him a full sick day, but I didn't; I'm not a monster. But what about Thursday, the day he died?

"Oh, that's a sick day, Mr. Shirley, no doubt about it," but let me give you all the information, ok? By Thursday, Michael only had half of a sick day left, but he was out *all* day, you know, dying. A half-sick day can't cover a full day. You don't need an MBA from Harvard to figure that one out. So, what about Michael's vacation days? Unfortunately, he requested the remainder of his days for a vacation in August. Would he want to use one of those days from August and use it to cover last Thursday when he died? Did anybody speak with Michael about that? Seriously. I need to know if he addressed this to anyone before he departed from his mortal coil. Payroll is really on my nuts about this. I'm two shakes shy of having a séance in the breakroom just to get the answer to this mystery, no joke. God, he really fucked me on this. Us! Fucked *us.*

Oh, I can't believe he's gone! I'm sorry that Michael's coworkers were unable to make it today, but instead they're back at the office tracking down those missing reports that I pray some of you have some knowledge about. You might think it's cold of us to only send one person from the office to this funeral, but everyone would have been able to attend if this funeral could wait until Saturday like I advised Michael's parents, but that's fine. That's just fine. Shoot, the way this week is going we might have to come in on Saturday too, who knows.

Anyway, I'll be hanging around for the rest of the afternoon if anyone wants to tell me about Michael's final words concerning either the phantom T.P.S. Reports or how he wanted to spend his last sick day. I'll leave my card on the casket.

The Self-Published Acceptance Letter

Dear Mr. Michael,

Well, you magnificent bastard, you did it. Your manuscript titled "Ask Me About My Grandcats," has been carefully self-reviewed and is being greenlit for self-publication. Congratulations!

I'll bet you never thought this would happen, not in your wildest dreams, but it did! And who thought you couldn't do it? What publishing house actually had the *gall* to reject *you?* Well, all of them, actually. They all thought you couldn't do it, but you showed them! You're making your own waves now, baby!

Oh, my god, are they ever going to be sorry for passing you over!

Now, Michael, you might be thinking, Hey. Maybe I shouldn't do this. Maybe this is just a huge scam. Maybe self-publishing shouldn't be so expensive. Maybe I really don't have the talent for major publication. Michael, don't be an idiot. You're just scared. You're scared of being so successful your tits are going to fly off-- and that's okay!

Let's put your rejections in perspective: many great works were rejected all too frequently at first. Hemingway's The Sun Also Rises, Stephen King's Carrie, Joyce's Dubliners...all subject to frequent rejects. Shoot, even The Diary of Anne Frank was rejected 15 times before being published. 15! That poor girl. Can you imagine anything worse than having your own diary read and rejected by complete strangers? She must have been so totally embarrassed. Oh, my god, I would just die if that happened to me. I mean, I personally can't imagine anything worse than that, can you? But now, right up there with Melville's Moby Dick and Kipling's The Jungle Book comes Jenkins's oft-rejected *Ask Me About My Grandcats.*

Catch-22, Slaughterhouse V, The Great Gatsby, 1984, and *Ask Me About My Grandcats.* Can you spot the phony? Can you find which one is not like the others? I certainly can't. They're all masters of the quill!

Jesus, you're handsome.

The question now, Michael, is: are you ready for your life to completely change? This is what you've been waiting for since you were a young boy (after your dreams of professional ventriloquism were dashed by termites and family shaming) and now all the hard work of your writing life is coming to fruition. After reading your manuscript, I can see that your ideas are crisp, the tone is sharp, and your similes are as awesome as like, anything.

As far as rewrites and edits are concerned, I see the need for absolutely none. This book, like you, is perfect. And sexy as all hell.

So, I think before we get into the ins and outs of this publishing venture, we first need to take a decent author photo for the back of the book. Something that encapsulates your charisma, sex appeal, and willingness to disregard all professional and personal advice to not publish this work. Say, what about that one where you were in the tree wearing that Superman cape when you were six? Perfect.

Because after your book hits the shelves of your local parents' house, you're going to be very recognizable and famous. It's okay, don't fight it; it comes with the territory of greatness. And with that same territory comes childhood fantasies brought to life.

For instance, guess who read your book and wants to be all over you? That's right, esteemed Hollywood actress Karen Allen 1987. The beautiful blue-eyed brunette in between the years of 1984 and 1988, smack-dab in the middle of her roles in *Starman* and *Scrooged*. Jesus, what a fox. Well, she read that part in Chapter 6 of your book where you dressed as WWF star The Ultimate Warrior before asking for a raise from your boss and she instantly fell in love with you. No, I'm not kidding! Karen Allen 1987—yours. Don't ask how she ever got around to even finding your book, just...she did, okay? She found it and read it and now she loves you. Unconditionally.

Remember how they all laughed at you when you proposed the idea of Karen Allen being with 5-year-old you? Well, who's laughing now?

That's right, you are! And you know who's laughing along with you? Steve Martin. Why? Because he's in town and wants to meet you personally, that's fucking why! You're exchanging witty banter back and forth with the one and only Wild and Crazy Guy! Do you remember, as a boy, you secretly hoped to get incurable cancer so you could meet Steve Martin through the Make-a-Wish Foundation just to have this lunch? But getting to meet Steve Martin in this manner is so much better because you know what's greater than receiving Steve Martin's pity? Receiving Steve Martin's *respect.*

Also, not having incurable cancer is pretty sweet too.

The lunch might segue itself to a visit to the local museum where you and your new pal Steve will talk about intellectual, artistic things and people will see you two walking and talking and say to themselves, "There goes Mike and Steve. What a couple of chuckleheads, always laughing. Thick as thieves, they are!"

Steve will probably want the afternoon to carry the banter into a sit-down dinner, but you'll have to cut it short. "I'm sorry, Steve," you'll say, because at this point you're on a first-name basis, "I'm sorry, but I have to get back to Karen Allen 1987; she starts to worry after a while."

Steve will understand. And so will Karen Allen 1987; she's well aware of how Steve can sometimes carry on a bit too long when it comes to matters of art and philosophy.

Michael, you might be in disbelief that all of these things can happen, but they will; they surely will. But it's going to take a lot of work and it's going to take a lot of sacrifice, which is something I doubt you are lacking. But I know you: you're going to need a spark. Something to really push you into becoming the literary juggernaut I know you to be.

So, for tomorrow, why don't you go into work and ask Mr. Shirley for a minute of his time. You may then proceed to respectfully pee all over his desk. You can't risk the idea of being able to crawl back if this writing thing fails. You need to go nuclear. Now, I'm not asking you to defecate on his desk or anything (I know how you feel about pooping in public), but take a quick pee. And, you know, mock him a little bit while you do it. Make fun of his goatee and dead tooth as you spray a thick, ropey, dehydrated pee all over his oak desk. Tell him you've seen him picking his nose and wiping it underneath his desk, you know, the desk you're peeing on. Tell him you wouldn't let him manage your own sock drawer, let alone a multi-million dollar company.

Oooo, that's good! Use that.

Hey, I didn't say this was going to be easy, but trust me: you're going to need those 8 hours every day to sign books and accept praise from your legions of fans.

Michael, I look forward to seeing your work on bookshelves throughout your parents' house. Also, after all this is over, you should probably move back in with your parents.

ASK ME ABOUT MY GRANDCATS